# Land's End to John O Google

## Roy's Mad Adventure

First published 2014

© 2014 Royston Wood

The Moral right of the author has been asserted.

# Dedication

This book is dedicated to my long suffering wife and one person Remote Support Unit. Without her support looking after the kids, the dogs, the cat, the guinea pigs, the fish and the house (whilst also working) I would not have been able to complete this ride. Her commitment ~~is long overdue~~ is not only throughout my nine day absence from home for the ride itself but also for the frequent day long training rides leading up to it.

Beyond having to deal with all the day to day things normally shared between two, she also has to offer me mental support by phone and text and keep my blog going during the ride.

And let's be honest, I wasn't much use to anyone for my first few days back either.

# Contents

If you would like to follow the route ridden in this book you can download the route file here:

https://docs.google.com/file/d/0B3-Rtk-1DBnSdV9SRUdzNFBySHM/edit

# Chapter One

## Distinctly Naff Feeling

DNF.

Three letters. Just three little letters. Three tiny little letters.

But there they were, sat next to my name: Did Not Finish!

Defeat 'N Failure. That's what they meant to me.

Of course, that's not what they really meant. No. They actually stood for Damn (k)Nee Failed. But, physical incapacity aside, it felt like Defeat 'N Failure.

Staring hard at the screen, where the results for the London Edinburgh London (LEL) Audax cycle were posted, I raged internally against the cruel twist of fate that had put me in this position. If I'd been ten seconds later (or earlier) this wouldn't have happened. Or if I'd just taken a different route home that day. Or if the bloody lorry driver had kept his eyes open!

I took a breath to calm down. I was being melodramatic. Why would I have taken a different route home? I always cycle that way. And if I was ten seconds earlier or later then I might have been hit by something else and damaged more severely. What had happened had happened. I couldn't change it. It was fate. Kismet.

Bollocks: I don't believe in fate. If fate exists, what is the point of having free thought? Where is the benefit in having choices if everything is predestined? And surely my destiny was to complete the ride. A mere lorry knocking me off my bike shouldn't have stopped that. Destiny Not Fulfilled!

OK. That's definitely melodramatic.

Time for a cup of tea. Well, coffee. Decaf.

Waiting for the kettle to boil I wondered about the wisdom of setting myself the challenge in the first place. It had seemed like a good idea back in the depths of winter: something to set my sights at; a goal to focus on; a target to aim at; and any other cliché you can think of. Really it was an excuse to bugger off on my bike and ignore my responsibilities for a while.

For a while? Five days to be more precise. In a nutshell, entrants to LEL have five days to ride from London to Edinburgh and back again; a distance of just over 1410km or about 875 miles. Dotted along the mapped route are several check in points where food and, in some cases, sleeping facilities are provided.

Being of the opinion that most people are quite sane, I figured that not too many people would be interested in riding LEL. When I Googled the ride I was amazed to find the world is full of nutters. Some cycling forums had been discussing the ride for over three years! Because of the logistics involved Audax UK, the organisation that runs the event, only holds it once every four years, like the Olympics. And like the Olympics it attracts an international entry. I was later to discover that 1,093 riders entered the event from 32 countries. 94% of entrants were men, providing proof, if it was ever needed, that women are saner than men.

My musing was interrupted by a high pitched whistle from the kettle: it had finally boiled. Our state of the art, stainless steel, rapid boil kettle had given up on us and we'd been making do with a tiny, stove top, camping kettle until we got around to buying a new one. We'd been making do for about two months.

Nursing my coffee I considered that the entry list of over a thousand could have been much higher. Entry was originally limited to 1,000 and, expecting a high demand, the organisers had announced that booking would open at 2 o'clock in the morning on a rainy Sunday at the beginning of January, a time that only the truly dedicated would be up and around for (ok, so they didn't announce it would be a raining; but it was).

Being truly dedicated I went to bed with my laptop and set the alarm for 01:55.

Just before turning out the light and trying to get a small amount of sleep before the all-important booking, I decided to log onto the website in advance, to save those precious few seconds when hundreds of people from around the world jammed the system. And lo, the booking was already open! A full three hours before schedule. Hoorah! Quick as a flash I booked, paid, logged out, shut down and went to sleep a happy bunny.

When the alarm went off the next morning I struggled out of bed and sneaked down the stairs, trying not to wake our two year old son. He has a hair trigger wake up mechanism linked to the squeaky stairs and I needed to get coffee inside me before facing an overly bright and cheerful toddler on a Sunday morning.

Waiting for the kettle to come to the boil I smiled

as I remembered that I was now booked on LEL. Then I frowned, thinking that I hadn't really ridden much more than 10 miles together for months. So I went to the toilet for inspiration.

In the toilet I dug through a stack of old Arrivées, the quarterly Audax magazine, until I found an edition with write ups of the last time LEL was run.

Pouring a strong coffee to get me going for the day, I sat at the kitchen table and read an article that made me wonder what I was getting myself into. As the rain hammered against the French doors I tried to think what it might be like to ride for five days, with very little sleep, if it was pouring with rain the whole time, which apparently it had last time around.

But the caffeine had kicked in by now so I was feeling positive and was buzzing with excitement.

By the time I had finished reading a second article I was starting to wonder where everyone else was. I glanced at the clock and had to double take. 02:34! I had forgotten to reset the bloody alarm!

I went back to bed and tried to sleep through my caffeine high. It didn't work.

It's funny when I think back to it, like a scene from a sitcom, but it wasn't much fun at the time. I've been drinking mostly decaf since then.

Finishing the last of my current decaf I glanced back at the laptop screen where my shame was still displayed. Definitely Not Fit.

Well, I knew that wasn't true: I'd trained pretty well and completed my first Super Randonneur series in the months prior to the LEL. That's a series of four rides of 200km, 300km, 400km and 600km, which sounds like quite an ordeal until you consider that

LEL was almost as long as all of those put together.

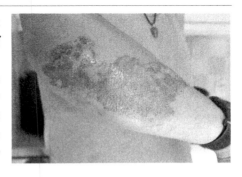

That is what was gnawing away at me. Was I fit enough? Did the injury stop me? Or did I just give up?

After putting in the training, just ten days before the start of LEL I was hit by an articulated lorry whilst cycling home from work in a cycle lane. All things considered I was really lucky. My bike was damaged, my brand new Sat Nav was smashed, my cycling clothes were ripped, my right forearm and shoulder had hardly any skin on them and my knee was swollen with damaged ligaments - but I was alive.

The thought of being alive kept me happy for a day or so, then I started to question if I could still do the ride. True, I couldn't put any weight on my right knee but perhaps if I got onto the bike I could pedal, pushing mainly with the left?

Two days later I managed to drag my leg over the bike and, holding a wall, hauled myself onto the saddle. Great! I clipped in and tried to turn the pedals. My knee wouldn't bend. I just couldn't turn the crank over. Blast! On top of the disappointment unclipping my cleat from the pedal, which involved twisting the foot sideways, proved to be an excruciating experience.

Two days after that I could put some weight on my right leg. I hobbled into the hospital to ask the consultant whether the ride was a possibility.

No. After ten miles the knee would become so swollen it would just seize up.

But would it cause permanent damage?

No. It would put recovery back somewhat though. It needed at least ten weeks to heal.

Well I didn't have ten weeks. I had five days.

Another two days later I put the doctor's theory to the test: I cycled to work, an eleven mile ride. Woo hoo! It was slow and awkward and painful but I made it without seizing up. In your face ten miles (as my sons would say)!

I made it home again as well. The next day I did the same.

Two days after that I limped to the start line (I still couldn't walk on it very well) and set off.

Without going into details, 24 hours later I was 250 miles north, as the bicycle meanders, in Thirsk, North Yorkshire. I was feeling crap and my knee was very painful and stiff.

I was at a particularly low ebb because I had been forced to walk up one of the hills in the last section of the ride. The problem was that I was using a bike with high ratio racing gears, because my preferred bike, with nice low gears, had been damaged by the lorry. The higher gears meant that I had to use a lot more power to turn the pedals on steep hills, a difficulty with my knee.

So I sat contemplating the next part of the ride. I was not at a standstill. I could still ride but having to walk up a hill was concerning. The hills to come in the next couple of sections were much more of a challenge that those I had faced so far. I did not want to get stuck in the middle of the Yorkshire Moors when my knee seized up and refused to bend.

Even if I got over the Moors I would then face the hills south of Edinburgh; twice, once on the way up and once on the way back down. At least one of those crossings would be in the dark. And after that it was over the Yorkshire Moors again, back to Thirsk.

There was no rescue service on the ride; each rider had to look after themselves. If I did abandon the ride in the middle of nowhere, my family would have to come and rescue me all the way from London. That was already 250 miles away and it would get further with every pedal stroke. If my knee seized up just south of Edinburgh it would be an 800+ mile round trip. Not only would that be too much to ask of my family, it would also mean I would be struck in an exposed place for 6-8 hours awaiting rescue, possibly in driving rain

However, if I rode back to London, retracing my wheel rotations, I would be getting closer with every pedal stroke, so when my knee did give up the rescue team would have less distance to travel.

I sat and internally debated for about half an hour then got up, hobbled to the control and informed them I was cycling back to London.

38 hours later, including a very refreshing overnight in a B&B, I arrived at my brother-in-law's

flat in north London having ridden nearly 500 miles.

Hooray!

Not hooray.

There was a good side: I got to spend a couple of unexpected days with my family, who were staying with my brother-in-law whilst I was on the ride. So the positive was that I got to join in all the Londony things (except there was no theatre ticket for me and I walked around so much my leg swelled from knee to ankle).

But over those couple of days it started to play on my mind that it was not actually a good thing that I had made it back to London without assistance. That meant I could have gone on. By the time I had returned to London I would have been on the return from Edinburgh.

The more I thought about it, the more I reflected that if I had just stuck in there I could have made it. Then DNF would have stood for Did Not Falter.

# Chapter Two

## Doing the Sensible Thing

A couple of weeks after returning home my head wouldn't let go of the thought that I had just given up. The going got tough and I'd had enough.

Most people were very sympathetic and said all the things they thought they had to: 500 miles is still a heck of a way; you shouldn't have been cycling at all, idiot; I couldn't have made it up the first hill; look, you still can't walk without a limp so how the hell did you think you were going to make it? Jeez! (roll of eyes).

All very positive and supportive and I tried to take it on board and believe it. On the surface it was working. Even on the inside I was managing to construct a wall around the issue, sealing it up so it couldn't run amok. If I nailed enough warning signs on it I'd remember never to peek inside.

Then I went to see my chiropractor, an expensive habit I started up after going through a car's passenger window when the driver made a right turn in front of me (ironically it was a courtesy car supplied by the driver's insurance company after an accident the day before: a common factor involved there somewhere I think). When I told the chiropractor that I hadn't completed the ride he gave me the most honest response of anyone. Despite having seen me limp into his practice a week before the event he was genuinely surprised that I had turned back. He hadn't expected me to make the full distance. He had thought I would have been forced to stop after about fifty miles. But he was very surprised to hear I had turned around and ridden back rather than pushing on.

He had been privy to my training rides and how I had reacted to each one. He was aware that I had struggled on a couple of them. In particular I had struggled on the 600km ride about a month before the LEL. At the 350km point, after an hour's snatched sleep, I had sat in the control feeling exhausted and demoralised. If I'd had a 'Zap Me Home' button I would have pressed it in an instant. I didn't have one though. What I had were three options: call home and ask my wife to put the three kids in the car, drive 2 hours to pick me up and then another hour to taxi me to my car (parked at the start/finish) and finally another hour back home; cycle 50 miles back to my car or complete the ride, another 150 miles incorporating a loop into Somerset.

I took the fourth option: prevaricate. The route of the ride and the route back to my car were the same for the first 25 miles or so. That gave me a couple of hours in which to make a decision.

Inevitably, two hours later I was stood on a bridge over the River Lew in Hatherleigh, wondering whether to head back to Exeter the short way or the long way via Somerset. From this point the route started getting

 further away from the start/finish until it made the turn back. I had either 25 miles or 125 miles to go.

Playing on my mind was the fact that I wasn't cycling very fast. I might

not make the distance in the 40 hours allowed. On the other hand it was only an extra 100 miles, which sounds a lot but not when compared to the nearly 400 miles overall. And (pay attention here, this is an important bit) what would I do if 24 hours into the LEL I felt like this? Give up? I don't think so!

However, the sensible thing to do would be to cycle back to the car and go home. I shouldn't overdo it so close to the start of LEL. I didn't want to ruin my chances with a silly injury (ha bloody ha!).

Wavering again I was staring over the bridge at the water below when one of my fellow 600km riders pulled up next to me and asked if I was going to jump. That's what passes for wit in Audaxing circles. I told him about my dilemma: should I head back or go on?

Go on, said he. If you grind to a halt deal with it then, was his advice. I thought about that after he had pedalled on. It was true that rescue was still an option if I went on.

Then I remembered that I had left a bag at the last control as a bag drop, to be collected at the finish. So, unless I wanted to wait hours at the finish for the control to open or drive a hundred miles round trip to pick the bag up some time later, I had no choice but to finish the ride.

Decision made for me, I pushed on and dragged myself into the finish with about an hour to spare. Elated at having overcome my demons and getting to the end, I left the control on a high and drove home. It was only the next day that I realised I hadn't picked up my drop bag!

So, the chiropractor got out his wrecking ball and smashed my feeble wall down, exposing the truth for all to see: when things got difficult Roy gave up, using his dodgy knee as an excuse to stop trying. He wore his knee support as a disguise to hide behind.

He didn't say any of that. He probably didn't think any of that. But *I* did. He was echoing back the thoughts that had been leaking through that wall all the time. The more I dwelt upon it the more I came to the conclusion that I had done 'the sensible thing'. On any logical assessment of the situation the thing to do was exactly what I did. As a business decision it would have been the right one, with far more pros than cons. But that isn't what that sort of ride is about. If everyone was being 'sensible' there wouldn't have been hundreds of people disappointed that they didn't manage to get a place on the ride in the first place. Sensible people wouldn't even contemplate the ride: it was not a sensible thing to do. So why had I based my decision to ride back home on sense? Because I was tired, in pain and frightened at what was to come: sensible was my shield and I cowered behind it.

It wasn't impossible for me to have finished the ride with my damaged knee. And if it wasn't impossible then it was possible, even if improbable. I will never know if I would have made it or if my knee would have truly seized up. Perhaps it would have given up on the first of those big hills on the route and I wouldn't have achieved as long a ride as I did by turning back. I will never know because I **did** turn back.

# Chapter Three

## A Plan is Hatched

So I brooded.

I don't want you to think that I spent the whole time brooding. I didn't. I'm not quite that sad. Anyway, I've tried it and found there is just too much life to get in the way of full time brooding.

Nevertheless the negative thoughts lurked like white noise. Whenever the clashing and discordant music of life receded I could hear it like a nagging and irritating hiss in the background. It was annoying.

Over time my knee slowly began to heal itself and before long I could walk without a limp, if I remembered to (it wasn't that I was looking for sympathy but simply that the body gets so used to limping that it just carries on). The more distant the symptoms of my injury became the clearer it was to me that I had used the knee as an excuse to let myself off the hook. After all, it wasn't that bad an injury. The real problem was that I hadn't learnt anything from that 600km ride about carrying on and not giving up. Now I was having to live with the consequences. The white noise was getting louder and I needed to do something to switch it off.

The obvious thing to do was find some other challenge that would prove my manly toughness. Not to others, you understand, just to me. My confidence had been eroded and I needed to bolster it. I needed to achieve something I could be proud of so my mind would be satisfied and I could settle back into humble British modesty.

A cycling challenge was the answer, something to rival the LEL. Well, Land's End to John O'Groats is about the same distance. I knew that because I had ridden it (or at least the reverse: John O'Groats to Land's End) a few years previously. Then my route had been very direct but perhaps this time I could add a few miles. And if I completed it in the same five days as LEL it would be an even bigger challenge. Yeh! In your face LEL.

Brooding done a plan was hatched. All I had to do was nurture it and grow it to maturity.

I was in a good position to plan a cycle from Land's End to John O'Groats: I have written a 'how to' guide on the subject and also have a website dedicated to it (www.landsend-to-johnogroats.co.uk). Time to put my own advice to the test!

The first task was to get a date in the diary so that I had a target, something to plan everything around. That meant breaking the news to my wife. Still, it was meant to be a challenge.

That is very unfair on my wife, who has always been very supportive of my stupid ideas. In fact, when I broached the subject it appeared that she had been well ahead of me on the cure, albeit not the precise nature of it. She had expected some crisis challenge and agreed to the trip provided it fitted into our normal life with as little disruption as possible, which was fair enough.

So when? Well, I didn't want to ride in the winter and spring was too far away: if this ride was going to be a cure then the treatment couldn't come soon enough. It was now already a week into September and I figured if I was going to do it, then I needed to be on the road before the end of the month.

When I rode John O'Groats to Land's End it had taken me months of planning and training to pull the whole thing together. Although then I didn't have an excellent planning guide to help me and, in theory, this time I was already fit enough to do the ride. My fitness couldn't have dropped off that much over the past couple of months. Could it?

As it happens a pre-ordered but unexpected fitness test arrived on the doormat the very next day. Back in the mists of time, before my summer had been ruined by LEL (or more pertinently that lorry driver), I had booked a place on a sportive called Moor to Sea. I had completely forgotten about it until the registration pack arrived by post. The ride was three days away!

The event proved to be a stiff test: 112 miles over Dartmoor (and over and over) with 11,000 feet or 3,350m of climbing on gradients up to 25%. I admit to walking up a couple of the steepest hills (my knee was still only at 75% and I didn't want to put my recovery back any further) but was heartened at completing the ride well within the time limit. I also managed to drag myself up a 'king of the mountains' hill climb part way through the ride within the prescribed time limit. I was very pleased with myself until two weeks later the Tour of Britain used the same climb to Haytor for the finish of one of its stages and the winner (Simon Yates GB) rode up in about half the time I managed. But he didn't get a bonus pin for his efforts: woo hoo! (Although he did pick up the points jersey).

Satisfied with my fitness I formulated a plan:

- Pin down a date.
- Create a route.
- Find accommodation.
- Work out how to get to the start.
- Work out how to get back from the finish.
- Decide what I was going to take.

A simple enough list but even as I wrote it down complications immediately sprang to mind. My wife is always tells me that whenever we talk about planning something exciting or trying something new, I immediately pull out all the negatives and litter them in our path, making the whole thing more difficult. I can't help it: it's just the way my brain is wired. I've tried pointing out that I haven't constructed the negatives and that I'm just highlighting them at an early stage but by then I've already spoiled the whole thing, apparently.

When planning my John O'Groats to Land's End ride, the most complicated part proved to be getting my bike and me to the start line. I was riding solo with no support and the start was the other end of the country with few transport options. I explored trains and one way car hire but both were expensive and involved a long and tiring journey with overnight stays. Flying was a cheaper and much quicker option but my bike could only be taken as standby luggage, which meant a risk that I would arrive at the start without a bike. And even if the bike was accepted as luggage what would I do with a bike box when I arrived? I certainly didn't want to risk putting my bike in a plane's hold without a box. Eventually I hit upon the notion of posting my bike to the start and following by plane.

This time I was riding the other way so my most complicated bit was getting back from the finish. I could try the same trick but how was I going to securely package up a bicycle in John O'Groats? And where was I going to post it from.

Fortunately, through my website, I have come into contact with a company that has set up a service to cover this exact eventuality. Based in Inverness, the John O'Groats Bike Transport Company has spotted the problem for cyclists and now offers a range of services. In short, they will transport you and your bike between John O'Groats and Inverness, where there are many more transport options. They will also courier your bike to your home if you require it and can even arrange to have your bike couriered from your home to the start.

So, a quick call to John O'Groats Bike Transport Company to check availability, a few minutes online to check for and book flights from Inverness to Exeter, a second call to the bike transport company to confirm arrangements and my return trip was organised. Man I was boss moding this planning! [Another phrase from my sons.]

The next obvious thing to do was to tie down the other end and book transport to the start. But something was telling me to stall on that; I don't know what, gut instinct maybe. Anyway, getting to the start wouldn't prove difficult. In the worst case scenario I could cycle to Land's End, it is only 100 miles away from home. I wanted to get on with the fun part: creating a route.

My previous route was going to be of very little help. I had selected that route to make sure I could cover as much road as possible every day. I had ridden the distance in six days and, not being a particularly fast cyclist, I had created a route that was direct with as few interruptions as possible. As a result the route was predominantly main road.

I did not want to ride main roads this time for two reasons. Firstly, the last trip had proved to be very boring for large chunks of the time. Secondly, despite cycling it length, I didn't really see much of the country. Well, I did, but the views from main roads are fairly samey and rarely inspiring. Thirdly, since my experience with the lorry I was very nervous about large metal things approaching me from behind. And lastly, I just wanted to enjoy the ride, not feel that hectic pressure of grinding out the miles, watching the clock, worrying about getting to the end of each day with enough time to recover before the next.

It is probably clear where I was going wrong: that was more than two reasons. Never mind. I wasn't really counting. I was too excited about getting out the road atlas and starting to plot a course.

Hours later I was slumped in my chair nursing a headache, defeated by the atlas. It is funny that I had forgotten what a pain it had been trying to select a route the last time around. And that had been simple compared with this. Main roads are easy to see and the biggest difficulty had been routing between them, when some areas had looked a little too risky. Trying to use minor roads was a nightmare. There were thousands of them and I had no idea what 95% of them were like. In Devon, if you head off the main roads you can be guaranteed of twice the climbing, the quieter the road the steeper the hills. Was that the same everywhere?

Well, I didn't want to be on main roads so I would just have to factor in more time each day for the hills.

The next day, with a fresh head, I decided to take a new approach and start from the Scottish end, where there are far fewer roads. It worked wonders; I was slumped in a chair with a headache much faster than the day before.

The problem was, I didn't want to ride the same road through the north of Scotland as I did before. But every other route was much further and again I was risking much more difficult terrain. I would just have to factor in more time per day to cover the extra distance.

After another day of attempted routing I came to the conclusion that I should have reached a lot sooner: how the heck was I going to ride further, over hillier terrain and in less time than I did last time if I wanted any chance of enjoying myself and not feeling 'that hectic pressure of grinding out the miles, watching the clock, worrying about getting to the end of each day with enough time to recover before the next'?

It was an impossible conundrum to solve so I didn't try. In a moment of clarity I decided to allow myself more time (there was no point making it harder than it needed to be) and to let somebody else do the routing. Genius!

How much time to allow for the trip was dictated by holiday and home arrangements. It quickly became apparent that I had nine days to complete the ride and get home. So, if I could get to the start after work on Friday then I could start on Saturday morning, cycle eight days to arrive at John O'Groats on the following Saturday evening and spend the Sunday travelling home, which was already organised. That gave me my start date and proved my gut instinct not to organise transport to the start earlier correct.

I quickly booked a train from Plymouth to Penzance for the Friday. I could cycle to the station direct from work (only about 1 mile) and then from Penzance to Land's End (about 10 miles). I managed to reserve a first class seat and a bike space for £15! I could have been transported cattle class for about £10 but I've never travelled first class on a train and £15 was a lot less than I had expected to pay in any event.

Now, who was I going to get to do the routing? Google. I opened Google Maps and asked for direction from Land's End to John O'Groats by bicycle. It took Google about 3 seconds to provide me with a route. All I did was adjust the start and finish points to be at the famous signposts.

Of course I was taking a risk because I was relying upon a computer to plot a course for me. Hilarious stories of satellite navigation disasters abound, such as cars being coaxed into the sea, potential 25 mile trips being routed several hundred miles via ferry to the continent and back or lorries being guided down steadily narrowing roads until they become wedged in. I would have to check the route before I set off but at least I could see from the map that it was heading in the right direction and wasn't routing me via ferry to Ireland and back (although that could have made an interesting route).

In terms of organising the trip that just left me with the accommodation to arrange. I'm the type of person who likes to know in advance where I'm staying. Not because I'm picky, it's just that I like to know where I'm heading and how long it is likely to take. If I didn't have anywhere booked I'd either stop too early, anxious that I might not get anything further up the road or I'd keep going until I dropped. It is one of the things I learnt about myself on LEL. I need to know there is a sanctuary at the end of each cycling stint, somewhere I know I am safe to stop and relax for a while before the next leg.

Although there were a number of organised stops where it was possible to sleep on LEL nothing was booked, which proved to create a sense of insecurity for me. This was reinforced once I reached the first sleeping opportunity and found that sleep was limited to 3 hours. I grabbed my 3 hours and discovered when I woke that many of the people arriving after me had found all the sleeping places taken. The eating area was littered with bodies comatose under tables, curled in corners or snoozing sat in chairs with heads cradled on bags propped on the table in front of them. I know this is all grist to the mill for many hardened tourers but I decided there and then that, given a choice, it is not for me.

So, I needed to find and book suitable places to stop overnight. I didn't want to be lugging a great load of camping gear with me, the weight would make the trip too much like hard work. Also, it would be October by the time I reached Scotland so the idea of being under canvas didn't have massive appeal. No, the best choice for accommodation was bed and breakfast.

Pulling the atlas back out I broke the length of the country into eight roughly equal chunks and started Googling for B&Bs near each day's end. Despite the fact that it wasn't peak season it actually proved quite hard to find B&Bs with vacancies that were open. It seemed that many B&B owners take their own holidays at the end of

September/beginning of October (or so they told me; maybe they just didn't fancy having a sweaty cyclist arriving after dark with a muddy bike and wanting breakfast at the crack of dawn). My options were also limited somewhat because I didn't want to detour very far from the route Google had supplied me with. As a result I ended up scooting up or down the route from each ideal stopping point trying to find available accommodation.

When I did finally get the B&Bs all tied down I amended each of my eight day's routes to start and finish at the requisite B&B. Now instead of eight roughly equal days I had a range of distances to cover from my shortest day at **99** miles to the longest of 140. The bad news was the longest day was the final one! I was amazed how much difference scooting up or down the route to find available B&Bs had made, especially in Scotland where options were sparser.

The last job on the planning list was deciding what to take with me. On my last trip this had caused a few problems. The temptation is to pile up everything you want to take and then find bags to put it all in. If you take that approach you will end up with four bags weighing 10 kgs each. A better way is to decide what bag you are willing to carry and then take things that will fit in it. Taking that approach on my previous adventure I had managed to trim down the things to take with me to the list on the next page.

The main bulk of the stuff to go in the bag was extra clothing. The karate slippers, long sleeved top and nylon hiking trousers were worn on the plane to the start and would be needed for eating out in the evenings. They were *light* weight but were *some* weight and took up vital room in the bag.

# Things to Take

1. **Me**
2. **Stuff to go on me:**
   - Tops
   - Leg warmers
   - Arm Warmers
   - 2-3 hour supply of food in pockets
   - Socks
   - Cycling shoes
   - Gloves
   - Helmet
   - Chest strap for heart rate monitor
   - Shorts
3. **Bike**
4. **Stuff to go on bike:**
   - Bike computer
   - Sat Nav
   - Lights
   - Bottles
   - Pump
   - Route holder
   - Day's route
   - Bag
5. **Stuff to go in bag:**
   - Tyre levers
   - Multi tool
   - Inner tubes x2
   - Zip ties
   - Chain lube
   - Plastic bags
   - First aid kit
   - Antiseptic wipes
   - Butt cream
   - Toiletries
   - Mobile phone
   - Camera
   - Various chargers
   - MP3 player
   - Batteries
   - Lock
   - Book
   - Wallet
   - Spare shorts
   - Spare top
   - Spare socks
   - Wind/rain top
   - Gillet
   - Sunglasses
   - Cycling shoes
   - Karate slippers
   - Long sleeved top
   - Nylon trousers

In the event, the only time I wore them was on the plane. This time the flight was at the other end of the ride so I figured I didn't need them until then. I decided to post clothes to the B&B in John O'Groats for the trip home. Space and weight saved.

The spare cycling top, shorts and socks were a luxury not used on the last trip. I had washed my kit every evening in the shower and dried it overnight by hanging it in the window. In October the heating would probably be on so I could dry it on the radiator, which would be even better. More weight and space saved.

MP3 player? Not used. Sunglasses? In Scotland in October? I could live without them. Anyway, they had been crushed under that bloody lorry.

I added neoprene toe covers and plastic cleat covers for my shoes, the former for warmth and the latter to walk when getting on the train.

The stripped down kit meant I could pack everything inside the bag, which was within the hand luggage dimensions for the airline. That meant no baggage to worry about.

When I cycled John O'Groats to Land's End the planning process had taken months but now I was an experienced pro. In addition, my own guide had proved really helpful in reminding me about the details that had taken me an age to discover previously that I had since forgotten, like how to get a route from Google Maps onto my satellite navigation unit (hereafter called sat nav). This time the whole planning process was completed within a week.

Excellent, Mr Wood: job done.

All I had to do now was ride.

# Chapter Four

## Metamorphosis of Purpose

Having nailed the planning in a week I still had a whole week left before the start. If I didn't occupy my mind I would start to worry about little details, like should I get the bike serviced, what was the weather going to throw at me, was my knee going to be strong enough...

I needed to do something positive to enhance the ride and keep my brain cells busy so that they had no time to worry. From previous experience I knew that a great way to use up hours of valuable time is to turn the whole thing into a charity ride. That way you can eat away time setting up blogs and charity donation pages, creating sponsorship forms, sending editorial to local newspapers, posting news, drafting begging letters, emailing contacts and so on.

The problem was I had everything set up from my last ride and it didn't take all that much work to amend the details for the new trip. By the end of the day the charity thing was done, apart from posting blogs.

My mind started to wander and it stumbled into the route. I was risking a lot trusting Google to plan a 900+ mile route for me. I have never had a problem with Google's routing in the past but at that time cycle routing was a brand new feature, still in beta testing. That basically meant it was being pushed out to users for them to find all the gremlins. In other words it could have been a right old hash up: it was expected that there would be problems.

Lifting the lid on my laptop I opened Google Maps and loaded up the route for my first day. On the surface it looked fine. Then I zoomed in a bit and found a couple of areas that didn't appear to be on the road. Mmmm? I would be riding a road bike.

Grabbing the little golden chap (I call him Oscar after the golden statue film award) I dropped him on the road at the point where the route left it and entered 'Google World'. Oscar is my favourite feature in Google Maps. He acts as a set of eyes at street level so you can see exactly what is there*. You can spin him around 360 degrees, zoom in and out and even whizz along the road with him. He is especially useful for checking tricky looking junctions or possible hazards. An added bonus is a feeling of familiarity when you get to the area on your actual ride.

*[I should add a word of caution and say that Oscar sees what *was* there when the photos that make up Google World were taken and not necessarily what is there now. Things change. In addition, the photos can have wide ranging dates sometimes making Google World a strange place to be. I have led Oscar down lanes which are in bright summer sunshine only to turn at a junction (and through a rip in the time/ space continuum) to find a bleak, frost encrusted landscape.]

Oscar revealed that the track looked to be paved. I pulled him out and dumped him on the road at the other end of the track. That also appeared to be paved. I couldn't whizz him along the track itself because the pictures he 'sees' with are all taken by a special camera carried by car, so pictures only exist where it is possible to travel by car. Instead I switched to satellite mode and zoomed in as close as possible to the track but it was impossible to tell what the track surface was like.

Checking the route for day two revealed that long sections were on a canal path. Again, it was not possible to see clearly what the surface was like.

By the time I had scanned the entire route I discovered that large sections were off road. Not proper off road but canal paths, old railway lines, shared paths and one or two sections that looked more like footpaths. There was also a river crossing which appeared to have no bridge and the route took me straight through somebody's house: "Open the back door, I'm coming through!"

Over the next day or so I debated altering the route to bypass potential problem areas. After all, I didn't want to get stuck, unable to continue along the route on a road bike. On the other hand it would take a long time to re-route and the potential problem areas might not be problem areas at all.

In the end the spirit of adventure (and an inherent laziness) won and I decided to leave the route as it was: I had a sat nav and if I became stuck I could re-route on the move. If I programmed in my B&B locations I could re-route by road to the end point of any given day if I had to.

The idea of traversing the country on unknown tracks morphed into an adventure in my mind. I started imagining myself as an explorer, trail blazing my way into unmapped (at least by Google Maps) territory. With a safety buffer of a couple of days before facing reality I was excited about setting off into the unknown, just me against whatever the track could throw at me.

Before long I was starting to think that this might be an ideal route. All those canal paths and old railway lines must be flat, traffic free and peaceful, apart from the odd barge chugging by. Most of the roads looked to be minor so whilst they may be a bit up and down hopefully they would be quiet. There only seemed to be a few stretches of major road and the positive side of those was that they would provide an opportunity to pick the speed up a little.

In fact, if I rode it on a road bike and proved that it was suitable, it might be worth writing up as a route for other people to follow. I had wrestled with routing and judging by the number of people visiting the 'create a route' page on my website, many others do also. A tested route could save people a lot of time and effort.

I would need to provide directions. The ideal would be point by point instructions at each junction, much like an Audax route sheet. Something along the lines of the extract from the LEL route sheet shown below.

|  | Place, Instruction | Signed | Road Name | LEG |
|---|---|---|---|---|
| 0 | ST IVES, CONTROL @ St Ivo School | | High Leys | 0 |
| 0.1 | 1st R | - | High Leys | 0.1 |
| 0.3 | R @ T [no road markings] | - | | 0.4 |
| 0.4 | R @ T | - | | 0.8 |
| 0.8 | SO @ O [by monument] | pedestrian zone | | 1.6 |
| 0.1 | R [opp Poundland] | (River) | Bridge St | 1.7 |

If I was going to produce something like that I would need to have some kind of blank pro forma sheet ready to fill in at each junction. That would be easy enough to produce.

Taking notes at every junction would take time though. I would have to note distance travelled, directions, any obvious signage, road names etc. The route notes would have to be accessible, preferably on the handlebars. I judged it would take at least two minutes to stop, check information, make notes and set off again. On twisty lanes I might have to make a hundred plus instructions for each day. That would mean two hundred minutes, over three hours of faffing around. That's not including the stop/go impact on cycling rhythm.

No, if it was going to work I would have to complete the directions as fully as possible before setting off on my bike. If I could get most of it completed I would just have to check the details at each junction and fill in any blanks.

The final days before the start were spent on Google Maps, painstakingly tracking the route and using Oscar at every junction to look for street signs that could aid navigation. Sadly it was not possible to read some signs either because the images were not clear enough or the automated software had pixelated the wording, presumably mistakenly identifying it as a number plate (which Google have to pixilate, along with faces). On top of that, Oscar couldn't head down any canal paths or old railway lines so some of these areas had a lot of blanks to fill in. But eventually a written route emerged.

By this stage, although I didn't realise it at the time, the purpose of the ride had changed. It had metamorphosed from a ride to overcome my demons to a charity come route guide testing mission. I had concocted other reasons for doing the ride so that I didn't have to admit that I had any demons, not unlike sticking your head under the covers. Instead of proving my manly toughness to myself I was now on a business trip to write up a publishable route guide, masquerading as a charity ride. Rather than a gruelling five day ordeal it was off on an eight day jaunt.

# Chapter Five

## And They're Off

The day came. Although if 'the day' meant the day I was to start pedalling away from Land's End then the day before the day came. But if 'the day' meant the day the journey began then – the day came!

In the pre-dawn gloom I hoisted my Carradice SQR Tour bag and slipped it onto the seat post clamp that would hold it behind my saddle. It was the same bag that had accompanied me on my previous trek across the country and on numerous other single day trips. It also gets used a lot for commuting because it is light (just over a kilo including the clamp – considerably less than a combo of a seat post clamping rack and similar sized rack bag), roomy, has easy access, is a lot more watertight than it looks, has a rigid structure and the added benefit of acting as a rear mudguard (it even has a wipe clean plastic strip on the bottom – unlike me).

The bike was already burdened with a Cateye TL-LD1100 rear light, a Hope Vision 1 front light, my Garmin Edge 800 sat nav and an impromptu homemade route carrier made out of Lego. I had also decided to put on tougher tyres: 25 mm Schwalbe Marathons. I would have liked a slightly fatter tyre, to absorb more off road vibration, but I didn't have the clearance between the wheel and my frame to accommodate more. Sadly, whilst more puncture resistant, the Marathons were about three times heavier than my normal tyres and the worst place you can add weight to your bike is the wheel rims. I won't go into the science but it is all to do with rotational mass, which really slows your acceleration and I would be doing a lot of starting and stopping on this trip.

Needless to say, when I picked up the bike it felt quite a bit heavier than normal. Still, I would be travelling a lot lighter than most people setting out without support.

Taking it easy on my cycle into work I quickly got used to the different handling with the extra weight. Things were sluggish in terms of acceleration but once up to speed the extra weight made little difference, at least on the flat. I would just have to make sure I didn't stop and start too often.

At the office I tried hard to get some work done but my heart wasn't in it. I managed a blog post and re-packed my bag after ransacking it trying to find my train tickets, which were in my wallet all along. I then made a final check that all my routes were loaded onto my sat nav. On my last trip, when I arrived in John O'Groats, the evening before the start, I discovered that I had forgotten to load them! Fortunately I had created them on a web based program and was able to download the saved files by borrowing the computer at the B&B.

After a final re-pack to find my wallet, which was on my desk, I wheeled my bike out to reception where a crowd of colleagues had gathered to wave me off. I thanked them both and pedalled away to the railway station wondering whether the other forty people in the building would even notice I wasn't there over the next week. Still, the faint hooray uttered by one of the throng was more cheering than the usual, "Bugger off then!" you get at the beginning of most Audax rides. I didn't want to set off from a waving crowd anyway: I would have probably overbalanced and toppled onto my side after my first pedal stroke. I've managed that trick in front of my wife and never lived it down. I don't need a repeat at work.

I was anxious cycling to the railway station. This was partly due to the still fresh memories of being smashed by a lorry as I negotiated the heavy traffic and partly due to the journey ahead. Strangely I wasn't all that concerned about the cycling bit, it was the getting to Penzance on the train that concerned me. I'm not a good traveller. I'm the sort of person that gets up two minutes before a stop in case I miss it. My base level of assumption is that it is all going to go wrong. I find it hard to relax until I get to my destination, which is a shame because it should all be part of the adventure.

Arriving at the station I dismounted and struggled my cleat covers onto my cycling shoes. For the uninitiated, many cyclists wear shoes with cleats on the bottom which physically lock to the pedals. This provides a more energy efficient transfer of power from the rider to the bike, mainly because you can pull up on the pedals as well as push down (although you should pedal in an even circular motion but we won't go into that). Nearly all cleat designs stick out from the sole of the shoe and make walking awkward. The idea of the cleat cover was to give a wider, less slippery walking platform and to prevent damage to the cleat. I had never used them before but with no other footwear they seemed a good idea, although £12 for a couple of bits of moulded rubber was a bit hard to swallow.

Wobbling through the doors of the station I found it more like a tube station than I remembered, with automatic ticket barriers instead of a human guard. Then it struck me that I hadn't actually been on a train for about fifteen years. At least, not a mainline train; I had been on numerous steam trains when my older boys were in the Thomas the Tank Engine mad age group of 3-6, but I hadn't been to Plymouth railway station for a decade and a half.

After wrestling my bike from the jaws of the hungry barrier I clicked my way to the end of the designated platform to the area indicated for bikes. Sitting down I tried to relax in the weak late summer sun as I waited for the train, which rolled in eight minutes late. That was a big improvement on my previous experiences of train travel. As students my wife and I had used the trains a lot and I would say our experience was that most were at least twenty minutes late, often well over an hour.

I wheeled my bike to the luggage carriage at the very front of the train. Opening the door I found it piled high with a jumble of suitcases. I asked a passing guard where the reserved bikes went. He peered in, grimaced and suggested I take the next train. When I pointed out that my non-transferable ticket was for this train he shrugged and said the train was late and needed to move on quickly. I jumped in and started stacking cases in a frenzy. They all had Saga Holiday labels. I bet they didn't reserve a space. Grrr! After a couple of minutes I had cleared just enough space to wedge my bike in. There was nothing to lock it to, apart from suitcases, so I just had to trust to the gods to look after it.

I started to hobble towards the first class carriages, conveniently located at the rear of the train. The guard gave me the hurry up with eight carriages to go and I thought I had better climb aboard and walk through the train. Well, I tried but I couldn't get on. The train was packed like ladies of a certain age in the front ranks of a Take That concert: it was like trying to get on a central line train in the rush hour. If I had managed to winkle my way on board I would never have been able to make my way through the train: even Flat Stanley couldn't have done it, sideways.

As the guards started to slam the doors on the compacted bodies, writhing limbs escaping through open windows, I increased my pace to a lurch and managed to reach first class just before the portal was closed. The guard looked down his nose at me in my cycling kit, helmet and wobbly shoes and enquired if I had a first class ticket. I don't think he was impressed when I told him my ticket was of the same class as everybody else's (it wasn't gold leaf embossed or anything) but it did entitle me to first class travel. Fortunately he had no time for an argument and waved me on with a look that said, "I've got my eye on you chummy!"

First class was also packed but they don't sell more tickets than seats so it was only packed seating. I sank thankfully into my, for once, empty reserved seat as the train pulled away, nearly back on time after my athletic endeavours of running the length of the platform. Maybe £12 on cleat covers was a good idea: better than my bike arriving at Penzance whilst I was waiting at Plymouth for the next train.

The first thing of great note on the Cornish Mainline, as the track between Plymouth and Penzance is known, is the crossing of the River Tamar, which marks the boundary between Devon and Cornwall. Certain elements in Cornwall have long held that the Tamar should be 12 miles longer.

That way it would run coast to coast and cut Cornwall off as an independent island. Certain elements in Devon agree, and bloody good riddance.

The railway crosses the Tamar over the Royal Albert Bridge, designed by Isambard Kingdom Brunel and opened on 2 May 1859 by Prince Albert himself. Brunel died later that year and his name was then placed above the portals at either end of the bridge as a memorial. One of Brunel's last acts was to be carried over the bridge, laid on his back on a bed, to inspect the finished bridge.

Although I have lived in and around Plymouth for over half my lifetime I have never travelled over the Royal Albert Bridge and as I rumbled over it for the first time I wondered at its construction. It is strange how you can have engineering marvels on your doorstep and never really think about them. I suppose they are just part of the landscape, something you see all of the time and don't notice. Now, for the first time, I pondered how the central pier had been constructed, in the middle of the river. I couldn't really conceive of a way to build down to the bedrock without diverting the river; a feat that would take far greater engineering than building the bridge itself. I decided to try and find out after my trip. (With a smart phone I could have researched right there and then but I'm a bit of a Luddite when it comes to phones.)

I was amazed by the simplicity and yet audacity of the solution. An 11.3 metre wide by 27.4 metre tall metal cylinder was constructed and towed out into the middle of the river where it was anchored vertically to the riverbed. The water was then pumped out and workmen descended inside to construct the pier from massive stone blocks. Once the pier was above water level the cylinder was removed. The scale of the engineering just to construct the cylinder is beyond me and that was just a throw away tool!

My journey through Cornwall followed the same theme with me marvelling at the massive amount of engineering skill and industry needed to drive this Cornish Mainline across a countryside determined to throw obstacles at it. Levelling the rollercoaster landscape had required a constant succession of high viaducts and deep cuttings carved through the hill sides to tame the geology. It would be an amazing feat today but the line was constructed before the invention of heavy machinery, relying mainly upon muscle and sinew. I hoped that the Cornish road builders had spent as much time and effort but knew from painful experience that they hadn't. Road builders in the south west tend to just lay the tarmac straight up and down the hills resulting in lots of short, sharp ups and downs, both physically and mentally for the cyclist.

On arrival at Penzance I found the luggage coach empty apart from my bike, discarded on its side on the floor. Obviously the Saga Holiday operator had just yanked out the cases at their destination and left my bike to topple to the floor. Luckily the only damage was a twisted handle bar which was swiftly corrected.

Switching on the sat nav I loaded up the route to get me to my overnight stop at Land's End Hostel and B&B. Hmmm? The start didn't seem to be at the station. I cycled around the car park and failed to pick the start up so I headed around the back. When I did pick the route up it sent me in the opposite direction so I had to tack across the traffic. Not a brilliant start but a start none the less.

The ten miles to Land's End were not as hilly as I

had remembered them from my trip four years earlier but then I had cycled the length of the country and was feeling a little jaded.

I decided to head to the signpost before stopping for the night so that I could take the obligatory photos. The weather forecast warned of rain in the morning and I was hoping to set off early so the light might not be at its best then. When I stopped I realised why the ride from Penzance had been so easy: the wind was strong enough to almost push me over.

These days the main signpost is removed at night. The signpost is leased by a local photographer who makes a charge for taking an official photograph. There is a permanent mini signpost to the side of the main signpost site where people starting or finishing out of hours can take their own photographs. If they can work out how.

Propping the bike against the signpost I leant into the wind as I tried to decipher how to set the self timer on my camera. This was just the sort of thing I should have worked out in the comfort of home, not in a howling gale as the light was rapidly failing. Eventually I had it set. Placing the camera on the footing for the main signpost I posed in front of the mini one. As it bleeped through its countdown the wind blew it over and it took an excellent picture of the sky. It tried again but achieved similar results with a picture of the stone signpost footing. Borrowing a bit of the low dry stone wall behind the signpost to buttress the camera I tried again with greater success but I was at a 45° angle and by now my smile was becoming fairly forced.

Thankfully a fellow end to ender arrived and we helped each other out with photos. He was also setting off the next day and was amazed that all I had was one small bag. Apparently he had a support car full of kit. I felt quite chuffed. In fact his photo clearly shows the sun shining out of my...

Pedalling up the slight rise away from Land's End I wished my bag was even smaller. I was grinding a very low gear into the strong headwind making my way to the turn that would lead me a short distance to my night's accommodation. The same wind was forecast for at least the next couple of days and would make the ride through Devon and Cornwall interesting. Day one was 120 miles. At the speed I was managing it would take about 15 hours, without stops!

There was nothing I could do about it, I'd just have to roll with the punches. Hopefully the weather gods would smile upon me and the wind would be lighter in the early morning and I could get a few miles in before it picked up. Maybe they could even keep the forecasted rain away. If they were benevolent they might share it with more parched areas, we'd had pretty much solid rain for the past two weeks.

My host swiftly appeared in the flesh and secured my bike before leading me into the property. The first thing that struck me was the half room, wall sized mural depicting the famous Land's End signpost. I could have saved myself the 1/4 mile trip to the actual

site and taken my photo right here! Without the wind. I trundled up to Land's End Hostel and B&B and stopped at the start of the driveway. It was thick gravel, not the skinny wheeled cyclist's best friend. I wheeled my bike across the grass verge and entered through the gate into a courtyard, where I let my host know I had arrived via the intercom.

I was shown around the accommodation which was hostel like, with basic but comfortable and well decorated rooms, a shared kitchen and a number of bath/shower rooms which were spotlessly clean and well maintained. They also provided plenty of hot water, a boon to the recovery powers of the tired cyclist.

An inspired idea was the Breakfast in a Basket. I was provided with a basket to fill with breakfast items that I could serve myself, using the kitchen facilities, at whatever time I chose to rise in the morning. On my previous jaunt across the country I had left before breakfast was served every day. This arrangement would have been much better than having to eat energy bars from my pocket.

After a goodnight call home it was time to get my head down. Getting it down was easy, getting it to shut up proved more difficult.

# Chapter Six

## Day 1 - The Road Less Pedalled

The bed proved to be very comfortable and I slept well, despite my nervous excitement at the prospect of setting off on a 950 mile journey. At least I did once I finally dropped off.

I had suffered from the usual night before apprehensions augmented with concerns about how much time I would lose checking the route sheet. Day 1 was one of my longest days at approximately 125 miles and I knew it would also be one of the toughest, if not the toughest, in terms of terrain.

As usual I had gained nothing by worrying. I would just have to start the ride and see how it went.

My host had told me that there was only one other guest staying at the hostel, a fellow end to ender. He must have arrived after I had turned in and wasn't awake yet so I was very conscious of making noise. As I moved around in the dark of pre-dawn every sound echoed due to the tiled floors throughout. I even took my torch to the toilet to avoid switching on the light because the extraction fans were quite noisy and I didn't want to wake anyone at 5:45.

It must have taken me a while to sneak around getting and eating breakfast because I only set off on my bike an hour later at 6:45. Even then the sun wasn't up and the light was gloomy so I set my front and rear lights to flashing. But, hopefully, taking the time to devour all those slow release calories would see me through the first couple of hours of cycling.

Wheeling my bike back over the grass to the road I decided it was pointless cycling back to the signpost in the dark. It wasn't like there was a crowd of supporters and well-wishers waiting there to give me a big send off. I'd done this before, starting out from John O'Groats, and there is a profound sense of loneliness at the start line. There is no one there but you. After months of planning you feel there should be some kind of starting gun and a general waving of flags. Even, an Audax style, "Bugger off then!" would be better than the, "Oh well, better get going then," that echoes in the cavern of your own head, emptied by nervous anticipation. There's an out of body feeling, like going into an exam, because your mental has retreated, not quite believing that your body is doing this. The body works okay on autopilot for a while and you can relax and watch, until you hit the first instruction on your route and you have to rush back to reality.

Skipping the 'start line' I avoided all that. Clipping into the pedals I gave my first push down on the cranks and was away. But I was only off to join the ride, not really starting it. The mental weight of expectation and responsibility was considerably less. And I'd saved myself ½ a mile of pedalling.

The first couple of hundred metres were fantastic, cruising with a massive cross tailwind. Then I turned east, directly into the wind and almost ground to a halt. As I had hoped for, the weather gods were smiling on me but it was a malicious grin, full of the promise of strong headwinds and rain. There nothing for it but to find a low gear and twiddle into the wind. This was not ideal, twiddling, like piddling, is best done with the wind, not against it.

On my way from the railway station to Land's End I had cycled along the A30 but my route turned off onto a narrow lane to follow National Cycle Route 3 after about a mile and a half. Immediately I gained the wind baffling benefit of hedges. This was countered by an increase in the gradient but on such a windy day I felt I had the best of the deal.

Although the main road was devoid of vehicles this early in the day it was pleasant to be cruising along a single track lane. The sinuous tarmac had a profound calming effect as it snaked its way through the countryside, if you ignored the sound of the wind ripping the tops off the hedges. Any initial nerves were easing out of my body and I could feel the normal adrenaline rush experienced at the start of any ride subsiding.

When I had sent Oscar down this lane on Google Maps whilst planning, the sun in Google World had been shining brightly and judging by the foxgloves in the hedges it looked to be about May. In fact, going back afterwards and checking, the pictures are dated May 2009. I can report that on 28th September 2013 it was not sunny and although it wasn't actually raining the weather had been particularly wet for the previous couple of weeks. As a result the local farmer had managed to distribute a fair proportion of his fields on the lane and conditions soon deteriorated. Instead of a narrow lane it meant I had two parallel, very narrow tracks of relatively light mud, separated by a ridge of thick slippery gung, to choose between.

All the lanes through to Newlyn followed much the same theme but with varying gradients, up to a maximum of 16%, and differing types of 'mud', some of

which smelt quite ripe. I was happy not to slide over and get any more acquainted with it than a bit of spray, or spread, as the term might be for slurry.

The ups and downs and the mud, combined with frequent stops to make notes about the route was already taking a toll on my speed. Not only that but the steep gradients up had me worrying about my knee and the steep, mud slick gradients down were already playing havoc with my shoulders due to tension and braking.

The lanes were charming but the conditions were not brilliant and I was looking forward to hitting Newlyn and a flat run along the seafront for a couple of miles.

The final descent to Newlyn Harbour was very steep and covered with moss. Fortunately it was dry. It would be treacherous when wet, especially with a blind T junction halfway down and another at the harbour itself. I made a note to offer the alternative route of the A30 to Newlyn if I ever wrote the route up as a guide.

The seafront was deliciously flat but with a sour aftertaste of bloody exposed. The wind was skipping straight across the bay, whipping up the white horses, with nothing to slow it down except me. Already missing those gloriously sheltered lanes I ground my way along the sea front and onto the cycle path that would take me beyond Penzance towards Marazion where St Michael's Mount beckoned in the distance.

Known locally simply as the Mount, St Michael's Mount is a tidal island linked to the shore by a man made causeway of granite setts, passable between low and mid tide. The land and buildings are now managed by the National Trust but historically were a counterpart of Mont Saint Michel in Normandy. The land was gifted to the Benedictine order of monks at Mont Saint Michel by Edward the Confessor in the 11th century. They established a Priory on the Mount although a monastery may have existed there from as early as the 8th century.

The cycle path started with great promise with a tarmacked surface but this quickly disappeared. For the most part the surface was a very rideable hard packed surface but there was a stretch of what could best be described as honeycombed cast concrete. I assume the theory was the holes of the honeycomb would fill with pebbles or gravel but they had not, or at least not fully. Suspension would have been useful

and I had to stop after the, thankfully, short section to make sure none of my bits had rattled loose. Happily they were all intact. Relieved I checked to make sure nothing had rattled loose on the bike either.

As I set off once more I did a double take as another cyclist went past in the opposite direction. I couldn't be sure but I thought I had met him on an Audax ride a few months earlier. It was a possibility it was him because at the end of the ride he had told me he was getting a train back home to Camborne, which is only 15 miles away from Penzance. But by the time I had computed all this it was too late to hail him to find out: he was already gone with that ferocious wind pushing him along.

Mentally I had been prepared for a stiff climb away from the seafront but was spoilt with some long gradual climbs through very pleasant, virtually wind free lanes. There were some surprises in the fields too.

Having lived close to the Cornish border for more than half of my life I have become accustomed to the peculiarities of the Cornish. However, what I hadn't been prepared for was the peculiar nature of the sheep this deep in the county. They seemed to have very long necks and legs (only two of these), small pointy heads with beady eyes and what looked rather like beaks. I'm not convinced their wool would have been highly sought after either, it looked rather feathery in texture. I took a picture to prove to myself later that they had been rhea-l.

With little muck and mud to contend with I soon tacked across the narrowest part of the peninsula to Hayle on the north coast.

Wheeling through town I wasn't sure how I felt

about the next stretch; 16 miles or so on the A30. Having taken me on a number of tiny lanes and footpaths I didn't understand why Google had insisted on shoving me onto the A30. True it was the most direct route and I had used it on my previous trip all the way through Cornwall. In fact it was the *only* road I had cycled on in Cornwall on that trip, taking me all the way to Land's End. But back then I hadn't experienced being hammered into the tarmac by a lorry. I was also painfully aware that there had been two cycling fatalities on this very stretch of road earlier in the year – end to enders.

However, I had vowed to follow the route to see where it went and that I would do. But I didn't have to like it.

And I didn't. The first 11 miles or so were on dual carriageway and not too bad because there was a thin strip of tarmac beyond the solid white line at the edge of the road that I could ride on, like a cycle lane. The only problem was that every time I came to an obstacle, such as a bridge, the narrow strip of tarmac disappeared, again like a cycling lane; just when you actually need it, it melts away leaving you in the thick of the traffic.

At Three Burrows roundabout I had to take the third exit. It was extremely busy and certainly got the adrenaline pumping. There is a cycle track that will ease you over the first junction but it doesn't lead over the second, back onto the A30; perhaps for good reason. The road narrowed dramatically to single lane and a fairly narrow single lane at that. That, however, did not slow the traffic. The strip of tarmac behind the white line was non-existent and there was very little room for the thundering traffic to pass. The only thing going faster than the traffic was my heart rate, partly for the exertion of trying to pedal my way through the section as quickly as possible but mostly due to outright fear.

I was very relieved when the 'safe' tarmac strip reappeared beyond the protective white line. Of course the white line clearly provides no protection at all but does give some kind of mental security blanket. Still, I breathed a sigh of relief half a mile further on when my sat nav led me off the A30 to much quieter roads.

If you removed all the cars from the A30 it would possibly provide the easiest cycling through the area. The engineers had at least attempted some mild form of contouring resulting in long but relatively gradual climbs and similar descents. With a tailwind you could whip along at a good speed, carrying the momentum from the downhill sections far up the following uphill (there are no real flat sections). But with a raging headwind it had been a different story. I had to pedal on the downhill sections to maintain speed and my momentum was ripped away in the wind the moment the slope levelled out, leaving me with no advantage when the next uphill section started a few metres later. So progress had been slower than I had hoped, despite not having to stop to make notes on my route sheet.

By this stage I was 40 miles in and the time was 11:10, so I had been on the road for nearly 4½ hours. That's an average of just over 9 miles every hour. At that rate 125 miles was going to take nearly 14 hours, which would mean a finish around 20:30-21:00.

My knee was holding up okay but my shoulder was getting painful. My shoulder was the reason for all those expensive chiropractor sessions. It was a recurring problem that had been exacerbated in my accident. In its own way it was as much a problem as the knee but at least it shouldn't actually seize up and physically prevent cycling; it was just painful. No doubt I had been gripping the handlebars a little too tightly for the last few miles. I took some vitamin I (ibuprofen) and tried to mentally release the tension from my shoulders. The rest of the day was on quiet roads and there was no need to stress over the time. I was nearly a third of the way through the day and had ticked off nearly a third of the directions so as long as I kept that up I should be at the B&B by 21:00.

Amazingly it worked. On my last trip my abiding overall memory was the feeling of racing against the clock to get the miles in every day. Up to this point, this trip had been much the same. From now on, with a few blips, the rest of this trip was to be ridden with a completely different mind-set: time didn't matter, there was no point chasing the clock. As long as I had time enough to

recover before the next day who cared how long I took; it wasn't a race. I should just relax and enjoy the ride.

The relaxing and enjoying was aided enormously by the route from this point in. In stark contrast to the A30 the lanes that followed were quiet, peaceful and beautiful. Being deep in nature I stopped for a call of the same name at a farm gate. As the pressure slowly released I stood gazing at a wind farm in the distance and smiled: at least someone was benefitting from all this wind. Thankfully, back on high hedge lined lanes, I wasn't being buffeted much either.

However, I was running very low on drink. Other than near the start, when I didn't really need one, I hadn't passed a shop all day. Five hours into the ride both of my bottles were as good as empty. If it had been a warm sunny day they would have been dry long ago. If I didn't come across a shop soon I would have to go in search of one, a detour I didn't want to make.

Although the lanes were glorious some stretches were extremely bumpy. I was juddering down a particularly lumpy but fast downhill when something pinged off the bike. I threw the anchors out and checked the bike to see what was missing. At first I couldn't spot anything but then I noticed that my homemade Lego route sheet holder had partially disintegrated.

A Lego route sheet holder may seem a strange idea.

That's because it is. But it was also very practical (apart from disintegrating on bumpy roads). Using flat plates I was able to make a custom sized board that was rigid, water resistant and very lightweight. It was also the only material I had to hand the night before I was due to set off when I realised that I would need one. Hopefully my eldest son wouldn't notice I had plundered his extensive supply before I could sneak the bits back.

Having worked out what was missing all I had to do now was find all the little bits of black Lego on the black tarmac road.

A few minutes later I had reassembled the board. It had been held by elastic bands to the rechargeable backup battery pack for my sat nav, which in turn was zip tied to the stem (the bit attaching the handlebars to the rest of the bike). To reduce the effect of the vibration from the road I wrapped the board with my reflective ankle bands before reattaching it.

The repair held up and the lanes became smoother. My route sheet went wrong though and I lost a few minutes trying to work out what had happened and making notes for amendments. Then a couple of miles later I realised that I was no longer following the blue line on my sat nav. By concentrating on the paper route sheet I had taken my eye off the sat nav. Either the sat nav was wrong or I had taken a wrong turn. Stupid sat naff! Stupid me?

A house nearby was proudly flying the Cornish Flag (like the

English flag but a white cross on a black background) so I knew I hadn't gone that far astray. However, I didn't want to backtrack and add the extra mileage so I zoomed my view out on the sat nav until I could see the line of the route. I then mentally plotted a course to intercept it a couple of miles up the road.

Happily back on course I was doubly please to find a petrol station with a shop. With 55 miles under my tyres I filled my belly and my bottles and pushed on.

A succession of quiet lanes led me to the Camel Trail. Don't get excited, there aren't any camels. It is named after the River Camel, which drains much of the north of Cornwall into that part of the Atlantic Ocean known as the Celtic Sea, off the north coast. The Camel Trail is a disused and resurfaced railway line running from Padstow to Wenford Bridge via Wadebridge and Bodmin.

Originally the railway had been built to transport sand to be used as fertiliser and was later used to move slate and china clay to the docks at Padstow and fish from Padstow to London. The last passenger train ran along the line in 1967 although it remained active for freight until 1983 when the need for expensive repair work rendered it uneconomical.

Part of the line is still in active use, reopened by the enthusiasts of the Bodmin and Wenford Railway

as a tourist attraction with old steam and diesel engine pulled trains to ride.

In total the trail is 17.3 miles (27.8 km) long and is used by an estimated 400,000 people each year. Indeed Cornwall Council, who maintain the trail, claim it to be the most successful cycle trail in the UK. I was only joining it for part of the 17.3 miles but the flat was most welcome.

There are a few places with old rails on the cycle track which proved to be slippery in the wet. I slid on one but fortunately it was at very low speed at a junction and I was able to put a foot down and avoid an embarrassing spill.

There were also fungi (I'll avoid all related jokes). I mention them merely because I had to stop to take photographs and it might seem strange to have a picture of them otherwise. And yes, I did *have* to stop. One of the many sad things about me is a need to photograph fungi whenever there is an opportunity. I have hundreds of photos at home. But we all have our quirks. Don't we?

I followed the Camel Trail for 8 miles, climbing almost continually at a tiny gradient. In total the whole 'climb' was 40m. Immediately upon leaving the trail I hit a 10% hill and climbed the same in the next 400 metres, which was followed by quite a bit more to climb up to the edge of Bodmin Moor.

After the tree enshrouded trail I found the stretch

skirting Bodmin Moor very exposed. I have ridden most of this part of the route a few times on Audax rides and have always enjoyed the open aspect of the roads. I wasn't enjoying it quite so much today. At one point I was struggling directly into the teeth of the wind along a flat stretch of road at 9 mph with my heart rate thumping away at 156 bpm. It felt like I was pushing up that 10% hill again.

Kamikaze sheep didn't help, wandering onto the road without checking left and right. I think the breed on Bodmin Moor is even dumber than the residents of Dartmoor. Twice I was nearly broadsided. They had also left a lot of slippery 'mud' everywhere.

Descending from the edge of the moor into the lanes took me out of the wind for the most part but there were other perils to face. At one point I rolled up, face to face with the legendary Beast of Bodmin Moor. Well, actually it was a black kitten in the middle of the lane but it was making itself large and hissing and spitting loud enough to fool the gullible.

I was almost out of drink again but knew from my directions route sheet (*84. In Whitstone R onto Balsdon Rd (by shop) 150.6km*) that there should be one soon. Thankfully it was open and I topped up for the last

stint into Devon, which I entered by crossing the Tamar (on a much smaller bridge than the Royal Albert Bridge) a mile and a half down the road.

Shortly after Holsworthy I turned off onto that section of off road I had surveyed in

Google World. My survey proved correct, the start was tarmacked. So was the end. But the middle bit wasn't. It was quite thick gravel. It was only a short stretch so I decided to walk. It seemed curious that the whole track was tarmacked apart from that short stretch. I could only think that it was a landowner issue.

The route followed the A3072 for a few miles; a fairly benign road between Holsworthy and Hatherleigh which I have ridden along a number of times in the past. After mile upon mile of tiny narrow lanes it felt like a motorway and I welcomed the detour the route took for a couple of miles to pick up a cycle track before spitting me back onto the A3072 to Hatherleigh itself.

As I had on the 600km Audax ride I stopped on the bridge over the River Lew. This time I wasn't despairing and fretting about which way to go. I stopped because I wanted to remind myself of the feelings I had suffered there before and to instill in my mind that I had gone on and that I had made it to the end. But mainly I stopped because I knew there was a bugger of a climb around the next corner; I had struggled up it after deciding to carry on the last time I was on that sodding bridge.

The climb was well worth it, providing a fantastic view. There were benches to stop at and enjoy it but the sun was rapidly disappearing over the western horizon and I still had 12 miles to cycle.

Descending the hill into Monkokehampton I came upon the scene of another Audax experience from earlier in the year. For there was the bench where I had sat and sworn as I fitted my second, and last, spare inner tube to my back wheel only 80 km into a 300 km ride. The alleged puncture resistance of Michelin Pro 3 tyres had completely failed in the wet conditions. I was forced to cycle back to the start rather than press on because I could pick up another inner tube in Okehampton and not risk being stuck with a flat and no means of fixing it in the middle of nowhere (which is a fairly good description of most of North Devon; in fact there is a town called Nomansland). My Schwalbe Marathons were holding up much better than the Michelin Pro 3s.

The light was rapidly fading and by the time I turned away from the route to find my B&B it had disappeared completely. By that stage I was tired and looking forward to stopping. The thought of a safe haven to collapse in had become a great comfort over the last few miles and the idea of having to press on through the night was repugnant. I began to realise that the LEL sort of cycling wasn't really for me. It was far more challenge than fun. No, a long hard day with a sanctuary at the end of it was more my cup of tea, or at least coffee – decaf of course.

As I ground up the steepest hill of the day I came to the conclusion that I was too soft for LEL but I didn't care: I was enjoying myself. Well, not actually right then, but generally. Right then I was cursing that the B&B was the other side of that bloody hill, which wasn't even on the route.

I had some lingering doubts that I was even in the right place at all. Google Maps doesn't always place thing where they actually are. It puts them where it thinks they might be, based on the postcode, and it is then up to the owner of the business to move the place marker to the exact location. When I had entered Google World to check the location I wasn't able to see the building itself, to see if it was the same as the picture on the website, because the driveway was so long it was out of picture from the road. So I twiddled up the drive half expecting to be chased off by guard dogs.

Fortunately it was the right place and there were no dogs, guard or otherwise, in sight. My host was very friendly and pleasant and keen to show me my room once we had secured the bike.

The B&B was a grand Georgian manor house with a magnificent double staircase sweeping up to the rooms, which were large and comfortable.

Over the last few miles I had been worrying about all the directions I had to check on my paper route the next day. Day 1 had 106 directions but there were 163 to check on day 2 and the distance, at 127 miles, was about the same. With that in mind I persuaded my host, who was very amenable, to provide me with breakfast at 7:00 so that I could get away early.

But tomorrow was tomorrow. Right then I just wanted to shower, eat and sleep.

I washed my kit in the shower using the treading grapes technique. This consists of massaging soap into the sweaty bits, in particular the pad in the shorts, and then dumping the kit in the shower tray, whilst you wash yourself. As you stomp around on the kit it acts like a washing machine. You then rinse the kit thoroughly, again paying special attention to the pad, and leave it to drip dry whilst you dry and get dressed.

Ah! Nothing else to wear. Didn't think that one through. Lucky it was a warm bathroom. Hopefully no one would come knocking at the door.

Never mind, on with the next step in the kit cleaning process. Once you are dried, wring as much moisture out of the kit as possible. Then spread the kit on your towel and roll the whole thing up as tightly as possible, wringing the towel if you can. Leave for a couple of minutes then unroll the towel. If you have been blessed with two towels repeat. You should now find your kit mostly dry. Now all you have to do is hang it in a slightly open window (if it isn't raining) or drape it over any convenient heat sources.

Food for the evening consisted of a Pot Noodle that I had posted to myself at the B&B (along with other supplies for the next day, not knowing when I would find a shop) and a handful of cereal bars. Yum!

Before sleeping I noted down my cycling statistics for the day from my sat nav:

| Distance: | 130 miles | Av speed: | 12.1 mph |
|---|---|---|---|
| Time cycling: | 10:40 | Time overall: | 15:13 |
| Av heart rate: | 143 bpm | Calories burnt: | 5,527 |
| Total ascent: | 2,463 m | Max speed: | 34.7 mph |

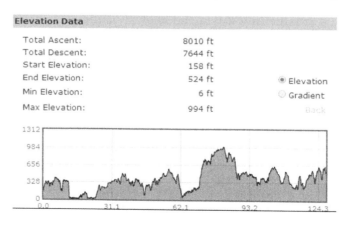

**Elevation Data**

| Total Ascent: | 8010 ft | |
|---|---|---|
| Total Descent: | 7644 ft | |
| Start Elevation: | 158 ft | |
| End Elevation: | 524 ft | ● Elevation |
| Min Elevation: | 6 ft | ○ Gradient |
| Max Elevation: | 994 ft | Back |

# Chapter Seven

## Day 2 – Hills and Canals

Day two dawned. Well almost, I was up just before the light at 6:30. I was feeling groggy and stiff but knew that once I was on the bike for a while things would loosen up. On my previous end to end my legs had felt steadily more leaden each morning but after a few miles they would be okay. True with each passing day the number of miles grew but they always recovered by lunchtime.

I must have been feeling apprehensive about the day because my first text home read:

*6:56 I'm up. Getting ready for breakfast. Today may be the toughest day of all. Might not get in till quite late if the route checking takes too long. Legs feel a bit tired. Have to wait and see how they are on the bike!*

Breakfast was served in the kitchen, which was huge. I felt sure my entire house could have fitted inside it. I'm not a breakfast person, at least not until I've been up and about for a couple of hours, but I knew I had to take the opportunity to eat as much as possible before setting off.

I sat with some trepidation in front of the ranks of cereals before selecting the sensible slow burner option of muesli. I poured a glass of orange juice and decided to start on that, in an attempt to wake up the taste buds. And perhaps a few swigs of coffee. I was sticking to decaf because I didn't want to suffer from an enthusiasm rush and burn all my energy early on, especially with the normal initial adrenaline boost pumping through my system.

I couldn't put it off any longer so with a grimace I dragged the spoon to mouth level and started stoking the engine. My body responded by demanding more, it was obviously in need. I dutifully complied and over filled another bowl with muesli and packed down a few rounds of toast, washed down with more orange juice and coffee. By the time the cooked breakfast arrived I was already near capacity. Now I know why it is called a 'full' English - I could barely move.

The strong easterly wind had not abated at all over night and it looked like I was going to be facing another day of headwind. In fact the forecast had the wind continuing for the foreseeable future but at least after today it would be more of a cross wind as I headed north. And let's face it, how foreseeable is the future when it comes to the British weather?

There was also rain forecast but at least when I set off it was dry. Yesterday I had been very lucky and had avoided all the rain. In the last 50 miles I had cycled over wet lanes so the rain had been falling but fortunately not on me. Perhaps those weather gods were favouring me after all.

Thoughts of weather gods rapidly dissipated as I turned right out of the drive and straight into the teeth of a 16% hill. A mile further on I ground my way up another, 15% hill. There was no mistaking I was in Devon.

My abiding memories of the first 20 or so miles to Tiverton were of steep hills (up to 20%), multiple stops to make route adjustments and poor road conditions due to mud and slurry spills. Looking back I think this must have been the toughest section on the whole trip. Of course I might have been feeling the effect of that massive breakfast, diverting the blood away from my muscles for food processing. And those leaden legs weren't helping.

It might also have been the effect of the rain which had begun to fall on my head for the first time.

Normally I do not bother much with protective rain clothing whilst cycling. Anything that is actually rain proof just causes you to sweat and, frankly, I would rather be drenched in rain than sweat. However, when planning the trip I had concerns about getting cold. It was October and the temperature could plummet, especially in Scotland. If I became soaked early on and had to cycle for 12 hours or so when wet and tired I could be in some trouble. I have strong memories of an Audax ride a few years ago when it rained all day. It was April and the temperature dropped to about 5 Celsius, not very cold but when soaked to the skin the body chills rapidly. At times I was shivering uncontrollably and began to hate the down hills, because of the wind chill, and had looked forward to the grinding up hills, which at least helped to pump some blood around. In the last 20 miles my hands were so stiff I could no longer change gear. At the end I discovered that the only other two finishers had suffered from exactly the same problem.

So, I was a bit worried about getting cold and had splashed out on a windproof top. It was showerproof as well but I was more concerned about stopping the cold getting through than not getting wet. I also bought a product called Rainlegs. These are like horse riding chaps. Made out of lightweight water resistant material they strap around the waist and hang down to just below the knee, covering only the front of the thigh. Again, my concern was not so much to keep dry but to have a wind stopping layer to help keep the large (although not as large as I could do with) muscles in the thigh from getting chilled.

At the first signs of rain I had stopped and put on

the top and the Rainlegs. After an hour of light but wind driven rain I was pleased to note that the top had kept me mostly dry and my thighs were equally dry, although the same could not be said of the rest of my legs. It was a positive highlight of that grim section.

It was with some relief that I turned onto the B3137 and descended the aptly named Long Drag Hill into the historical wool town of Tiverton; although after cycling predominately on tiny lanes all day the width of the road and the three cars that passed me made it feel like a motorway.

I'd been having some difficulties with the paper route in the last section but it was easy to follow through Tiverton. The only problem was that it led me the wrong way through the one way shopping precinct, which was an eclectic mix of the new and the old. In Gold Street the White Horse Inn looked Elizabethan and just down the street were some almshouses (pictured) even predating that. Opposite sat an amusement centre.

The almshouses were built for poor retired workers by John Greenway, a wealthy wool merchant of the town, in the 1520s. They are used as retirement homes

to this day although nowadays the residents don't have to pray for the souls of Greenway and his wife as a condition of residency. At least, I don't think so.

On the plus side the route directed

me onto a cycle path to cross the A396 dual carriageway, which saved me from having to take a 270 degree 3rd exit from a busy roundabout 100 metres down the road. Well done route!

I followed a cycle path along a disused railway for a mile out of town before transitioning along a short stretch of lane onto the Great Western Canal towpath.

The tow path had a good hard packed surface and was delightfully flat, if slightly exposed to the headwind. I felt a little cheated when after a mere mile the route headed me back onto the road and over the canal bridge. The canal path continued on the opposite bank but I did not: my route pointed me down the road.

Looking at the map afterwards I could see that the road cut out a loop in the canal, saving distance. As it turns out the short cut was well worth it, including as it did a back lane through Halberton that turned into a footpath between houses and back into a lane. At one end of the footpath stood a fine church and at the other a magnificent lane side pond.

The church had provided some bad news though: it was nearly 11 o'clock and I was only 27 miles into the day. Having been on the road for a little over 3 hours that meant an average speed of just under 9mph. I still had 100 miles to go which might mean another 11 hours: eta 22:00.

The constant stopping to check the route was killing my overall speed. The day before had been similar. My overall average speed had been 9.6 mph whilst my actual moving average speed was 12.1 mph. I had spent nearly 3 hours not moving, writing instructions (and, if truth be told, weeing a lot).

Back on the canal path I told myself not to panic; it didn't matter. I would make up time on the canal path, which was flat and only had a few instructions to check.

When it came to it those instructions proved to be needless, providing me with an unnecessary road detour of a few hundred metres through Sampford Peverell. On the approach to Sampford Peverell I was amazed to discover that I had been there before. Earlier in the year, on the National 400 Audax ride, my sat nav had died in the night and without a written route [stupid] I was lost, a few kilometres from the finish. Fortunately a fellow rider turned up and led me to the end. After nearly 24 hours of riding with no sleep he had misread his route sheet at this point and we had ridden a few metres along this canal before realising we should have followed the road over the canal bridge. And the rider who helped me out? Bizarrely the guy I thought I had seen in Penzance!

Unfortunately, whilst there were few instructions to slow me on the 5 mile stretch of canal there were other things to distract me by looking photogenic, like swans.

By the time I left the canal I was also being distracted by thirst. I was running dry and wishing I had stopped to top up my bottles in Tiverton.

I was cheered when the route tried to take me through someone's house though. Not literally through the house but through their brand new looking gate. It seemed that the owner had decided to build across the lane, which was probably private, and bypass the cycle route around the property (without signage).

There followed some ups and downs, the most notable being Nymehead Hollow. I thought this was a

natural gorge through the red sandstone, Cheddar Gorge not being a million miles away, but later research revealed not. According to that well known source of reliable information, Wikipedia, it was cut through by the Sanford family (although I imagine no Sanford wielded a pickaxe at any stage) to provide faster access to their home at Nynehead Court from the servant houses, which were situated in East Nynehead. They were either very philanthropic or extremely fed up with their servants turning up late.

I was happy to arrive at Taunton because I was getting desperate for drink but navigation proved tricky. Trying to get the paper route to read easily was taking a long time as it picked up numerous back lanes and footpaths. In the end I decided I would have to deal with navigating the written route through Taunton when I returned home. Instead I relied upon my sat nav, which was infinitely easier.

The footpaths and back lanes were traffic free but did pose their own dangers: they were full of undesirables. Not least of these were a couple of very dubious looking guys swaying about near the back entrance to Tescos, somewhere I really needed to get to. Taking a deep breath I cycled between them and they gently rocked out of my way, hailing me with the cans of beer in their hands. My tiny lightweight lock felt total inadequate as I clipped my bike to the bike stand, not 50 metres away. Tescos had conveniently located the stand just out of sight of everybody apart from my new friends.

I must be getting (more) cynical in my middle age because after a speed record breaking shop I returned to find everything intact. My buddies had slumped to the grass by this stage and seemed to be peacefully snoozing by the time I had loaded up and was cycling past them. Like true, dedicated drinkers they had managed to keep their cans upright to make sure they would have a refreshing drink to slake their thirsts when they woke.

The earlier rain had passed and, whilst windy, it was now a lovely sunny day. This seemed to have brought all the local drunks out to enjoy lolling about on the benches alongside the River Tone (from which the town derives its name – Tone Town). Although the benches were also right next to the Somerset County Cricket Club ground so perhaps the drunks had spilled out of there.

It was a relief to reach Firepool Lock, which connects the River Tone to the Bridgwater and Taunton Canal. The canal guaranteed me nice flat riding for the next few miles.

I stopped at the lock for a few minutes to reminisce about narrowboat holidays and the joy of locking. Nipping past on a bike was certainly going to be a lot faster. On one narrowboat trip we had chugged along solidly from dawn to dusk every a day completing a recommended 2 week loop in a week. We developed a locking routine which had us

preparing a lock in advance on locking series (one of which, Tardebigge, had 30 locks) to speed the process up. Being out of season the canal was virtually empty, otherwise we wouldn't have been able to do it but at that time we were the Lords and Ladies of the Locks and the swiftest barge on the waterways. When we got back in the car to drive home

it took us less than two hours to pass the furthest point we had reached on our normally 2 week loop.

It was lunchtime by the time I clambered back on to the bike and I was only a third of the way through the distance I had to cover. I was a little worried about time but the canal path had a really good surface and was reasonably sheltered from the wind. I pushed hard against the pedals and picked up speed.

The only things to slow me down were tired legs and canal bridges. I was to learn over the new few days that each canal had its own way of dealing with canal bridges

and locks. If you ignore the 'Cycling Is Not Permitted Under This Bridge' signs [☺], the Bridgwater and Taunton Canal offers the cyclist two choices: under the bridge, minding your head and being careful no one is coming the other way, or up, over the road and down the other side. I opted of the former, although I was highly conscious of my brother-in-law's recent experience of catching his handlebar under a canal bridge in London and ending up in the canal. The swans didn't look like they wanted company and to be frank, I didn't really fancy joining them, vicious buggers that they are. Even the cygnets will take your arm off.

Periodically dotted along the side of the towpath were concrete blocks with representations and information plaques about the planets of the solar system. The Victorians would be proud of the opportunity to improve one's mind whilst out enjoying a quiet walk or cycle.

Other concrete constructions along the canal were machine gun emplacements, relics from World War II when the canal formed part of the Taunton Stop Line, designed to stop an enemy advance from the west. Other defences include detonation chambers, now filled in with concrete and brick, which can be seen under some bridges.

Something else you will see a lot of on canal paths is anglers. Fishing is a favourite occupation on the canals with anglers using long rigid poles that stretch right across

the canal. As a result I needed to take some care and show some courteous riding. The anglers were very polite and seemed very conscious of not blocking the path so the least I could do was not whizz by at a dangerous pace.

With my mind on fishing I couldn't help but notice the electrical cables stretched across the canal that had been bedecked with dangling, brightly coloured balls. Having been brought up in a seaside town they put me in mind of the buoys fishermen use to locate their lobster and crab cages. I couldn't imagine what they were hoping to catch five metres above the canal though; unless they were fly fishing.

Before my wit could sink any lower, the canal terminated in Bridgwater. The next 15 miles of the ride, in stark contrast, was on the A38. As I joined the thundering traffic it was nearly 15:30, I was only 62 miles in, leaving 65 miles still to go with 70 more instructions to check. Despite the canal my average speed had plummeted to a little over 8mph which meant another 8 hours cycling, an eta of 23:30.

On the busy A38 I was making up time with no stopping and starting but I had to make a major decision: if I was going to enjoy this ride, which was surely the whole point, I would have to abandon the written route. I was losing too much time.

The tension in my shoulders eased when I turned off the A38, 50 minutes after joining it. Reversing the earlier contrast I was now on a very quiet cycle path. I had managed an average of 18mph along the A38. Although partly fuelled by fear, the increased pace confirmed my decision. I stopped to take the Lego board and route sheet off the bike and stowed them in the bag.

The cycle path was part of the Strawberry Line,

an on-going project to create a traffic free path from Clevedon to Shepton Mallet. It derives its name from the disused railway lines it utilises which were known by the same name because of the huge quantity of locally grown strawberries they carried.

As I neared the end of the line I was conscious of the ridge of hills looming ahead. The landscape had been virtually flat since Taunton and I started to mentally prepare my legs for the shock to come. But when I arrived in Clevedon my clever route had found the one breach in the ridge and with minimal effort I was through and cycling parallel to the M5 towards Avonmouth.

The route took me under and then back over the M5 via a footbridge and shortly later I was cycling around the security fence of a compound containing thousands of new, unregistered cars. It is a holding pen for cars imported through the Royal Portbury Docks, which can handle up to 700,000 vehicles a year.

I felt compelled to text home at this point because this is a well-recognised landmark for our family. We always comment on how they would never miss just one car, perhaps they could donate us one...probably just like everybody else driving past.

My text was timed at 17:48 and my distance at that point was 152 km or approximately 95 miles. That meant I had covered the last 33 miles in about 2 hours

and 20 minutes: an average speed of just over 14mph since I had stopped taking down instructions for the written route sheet. Woo hoo – good decision!

Whilst Google found a couple of interesting footpaths through the industrial landscape between Avonmouth and Aust, it mainly followed the A403. I had cycled along this road, in the opposite direction, on my previous trip and do not remember it being particularly dodgy. But perhaps by then I had become impervious to the threat of huge articulated lorries rumbling past my shoulder, having travelled most of the length of the country on major highways. This time I kept to the pavement, where I could, and made a mental note to try and find a quieter way.

The last 20 miles were on quiet lanes and after only a couple of miles I rolled by the B&B I had originally booked for the end of the day. My legs were very tired by now and I was regretting the date cock up I had made when booking which had resulted in the B&B not being able to accommodate me after all. The next available B&B was 20 miles further up the road. Still, on the plus side it meant a much shorter day 3. At only 100 miles I should get in early, especially without a route sheet to check.

As the sun slipped rapidly towards the horizon my shadow was stretching its legs, getting gradually further ahead of me as my own legs tired. The hay bales were also casting long shadows whilst the farmers maximised the daylight in the fields.

Said farmers had also been out with the muck spreaders. I had fun playing 'dodge the slurry splat' as the light from the sun disappeared to be replaced by the poor substitute of my bike light.

Fortunately I avoided any major spread flicking up and arrived at the B&B in a relatively clean and fragrant free state around 20:30. I had made up a lot of time.

My host was very welcoming and seemed to understand the needs of the cyclist after a long day: my bike was quickly secured and I was shown to my room with much chat but not impinging on my need for 'collapse' time.

The room was very spacious and comfortable with a magnificent view over the pond, although I only discovered that in the morning. There was also plenty of hot water to wash the dirt and the aches of the day down the plughole.

Most importantly I found a portable electric radiator in the bathroom and sparked it up to dry off my freshly washed kit.

The 'Red Cross' parcel I had sent to the B&B had

arrived safely and I opened it to pull out my evening meal. Same as the day before: Pot Noodle and cereal bars. Pot Noodle (other brands are available) is ideal because all you need to do is add boiling water and every B&B room has a kettle, even if some of them do take all night to boil a cup full of water.

Slurping down white hot noodles, I noted from the statistics on my sat nav how much less climbing there had been on day 2. On day 1 I had climbed 2,463 vertical metres. On day 2, despite travelling virtually the same distance, I had only climbed 1,168 metres: less than half the climbing and 70% of that was in the first third of the day, up to Taunton. The difference was reflected in my average heart rate being nearly 10 bpm lower and the calories burnt nearly a thousand less.

Less calories burnt or not I crammed some more in, made a call home and shortly after was dead to the world.

| | | | |
|---|---|---|---|
| Distance: | 131 miles | Av speed: | 12.7 mph |
| Time cycling: | 10:22 | Time overall: | 14:53 |
| Av heart rate: | 134 bpm | Calories burnt: | 4,614 |
| Total ascent: | 1,168 m | Max speed: | 32.1 mph |

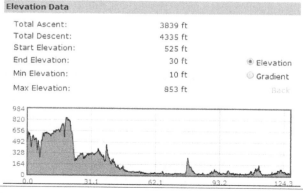

**Elevation Data**

| | |
|---|---|
| Total Ascent: | 3839 ft |
| Total Descent: | 4335 ft |
| Start Elevation: | 525 ft |
| End Elevation: | 30 ft |
| Min Elevation: | 10 ft |
| Max Elevation: | 853 ft |

○ Elevation
○ Gradient
Back

# Chapter Eight

## Day 3 – Bodies in the water

With only 100 miles to cycle and no instructions to compile I decided upon a lie in, with breakfast at 08:00.

Breakfast was a magnificent affair: lots of muesli, toast, juice and coffee with a sumptuous full English to follow. So good it deserved photographic evidence.

By the time I had rammed it all down and lumbered my bloated body to the bike it was 08:40; nearly an hour later than day 2 and two hours later than day 1. If I kept that trend up I would only be rolling away from my B&B on day 8 at 3 in the afternoon!

The wind was still brisk but had lost some of its teeth. Happily it had also shifted towards the south east, providing some assistance to my tired legs.

A mere 200 metres from the B&B the route took me over a swing bridge and turned sharp right onto the Gloucester and Sharpness Canal, or at least onto the towpath. The project to build the canal, designed to cut out a large and dangerous loop of the River Severn, began in 1793 but was so beset with financial difficulty

that it finally opened in 1827. At 26 metres wide and 5.5 metres deep it was the widest and deepest canal in the world at the time. Despite being able to take craft up to 600 tons it was only in 1871, 44 years later, that the debts relating to the build were finally paid off.

After a short detour by road through Frampton on Severn the route returned to the canal. I'm am not entirely sure why the route left the canal, there seeming to be paths on both banks beyond the turn off. Maybe it was simply to visit Frampton, which was, on the whole, very old and quaint. Although mentioned in the Domesday Book the oldest buildings looked, to my inexpert eye, to be Elizabethan and Georgian. Most of the new builds were designed sympathetically but there were a few naff bungalows dating from the 1960/70s, when regulations were not so stringent.

I returned to the canal, crossing one of the many swing bridges to the tow path on the opposite bank. Swing bridges were a feature of this canal whereas Day 2's bridges had been red brick hump back affairs. I assume swing bridges were used here because the width of the canal would have been too great to span with a brick construction.

As I contemplated comparative canal crossings the peace of the canal was disturbed by the violent scene of a game of swans mobbing a seagull. According to the Oxford Dictionary a group of swans is known as a game (unless it is in flight when it is known as a wedge). This particular game seemed to be rather unfair: 11 to 1 and that's not allowing for the huge size difference between a swan and a seagull. The thing is, whilst they look graceful and elegant, swans are vicious buggers (I might have mentioned it before).

For the first time on my route the state of the towpath deteriorated. Leaving behind the hard packed grit it became a narrow mud strip through grass. Fortunately it was dry, otherwise it might have proved

slippery. Even so, the mud strip was indented, worn by the tread of many feet and tyres, which provided a test of bike handling skills to keep in the furrow.

Fortunately after a mile or so the path improved. I could now take a hand off the handlebars to wipe the midges from my glasses. They were particularly thick along this stretch of canal, especially for so late in the year. A basking shark would have been able to cycle along with its mouth open, straining them through its teeth for a tasty snack on the move. But you don't see many basking sharks on bicycles. At least, not in this country.

Despite the tired legs I was making good time until I reached a road block - on a canal towpath!

The police had closed the path to deal with an incident. I pleaded sat nav dependence and ignorance of an alternative route but the helpful policeman gave me directions. I'm not sure if he was having a joke at my expense but his directions seemed to take me miles out of my way to bring me back to the canal maybe a mile further on. Only to find the canal path blocked there also.

I sat down with my sat nav and tried to figure a more direct route to the next canal bridge but found I was on the outskirts of Gloucester so all routes looked complicated.

Another friendly policeman asked if I was taking pictures. I showed him my sat nav and said I was just trying to work out a route. He gave me a, 'You'd better not be trying something funny,' look but also gave me directions. He then told me that I had better not be taking any pictures because it was a potential crime scene. I thought about pointing out that anywhere could potentially be a crime scene but catching his steely look decided against it.

I texted home instead. I do this regularly to show I am still alive. It also gave me the opportunity to smuggle my camera out and surreptitiously snap a picture of the police car, simply because the challenge had been set.

As I was doing this the BBC arrived and started chatting to the policeman. My straining ears overheard that a body had been found floating in the canal. It was probably a drunk that had fallen in (it seems drunks and canals must be synonymous) but the police were not ruling out foul play. I don't blame them, it wouldn't have surprised me at all to learn later that the poor fellow had been mobbed by a game of swans. [Please excuse terrible pun.]

The policeman's directions proved accurate and after skirting through a housing estate or two I was back on the canal which guided me through the rest of Gloucester and beyond, via the Alney Island Nature Reserve. Sat in the middle of the reserve is Thomas Telford's Over Bridge, a large single span stone bridge built in 1829. Despite not being officially opened to traffic until 1832 due to initial subsidence when the span supports were removed, the bridge remained in use until 1974 when the new bridge carrying the A40 was opened immediately north of it. It is now used as a pedestrian crossing and is preserved as the oldest large span masonry bridge remaining in England.

Back on country lanes I passed a sign to a Tithe Barn and decided to detour a few hundred metres to have a look. Access proved to be free (or at least there was no one around to stop me wandering in through the open door). The interior timber structure holding up the stone tile roof was impressive. I was later to discover that the barn was built about 1500 by the canons of St Augustine's

Bristol. After the Dissolution of the Monasteries the barn passed into secular use. It is now maintained by the National Trust, who acquired it in 1956.

Joining the route again I discovered another fine historic building a mere 400 metres down the road: Ashleworth Manor. Built circa 1450 it is a magnificent timber framed house with a television aerial sat incongruously on its roof. I had a chat with the goat and pony in the field opposite and they agreed with me that it could have been better disguised (I had been on the road, alone, for nearly 2½ days).

Leaving their company I started to hit some hills for the first time since Taunton. Not big hills but they were a rude shock after endless miles of flat. Realising I was pushing too hard I decided to eased off. I was feeling tired already and didn't want to burn too many matches early in the day. I had to think about the next day. And the next day. And the next day…

Fortunately I soon came to a sign which informed me that, 'You're nearly there'. Perhaps I had passed a hole in time and space and was now at the north eastern tip of the country. Great! But I would have expected more of a whoosh or a 'spinning through a tunnel of light' type of effect.

A few hundred metres down the road there was no sign of the Orkney Islands on the horizon so I guessed John O'Groats might not be the place I was nearly at.

Another sign appeared with 'slip road' on it. The line of my route on the sat nav turned rather optimistically down the slip road and crossed the blue line of the River Severn. Perhaps this was where I nearly was? Then I remembered spotting this on Google Maps and deciding to route around it once I got there. Well,

here I was. Perhaps I should re-route.

There was no mention of the word ford anywhere but as I perched on my bike considering how deep the water might be a canoe appeared and made for the opposite slipway. Whilst canoes are shallow drafted so are bicycles. The river was

probably a good 10 feet deep in the main channel. This was one part of the route I was not going to follow.

As I fiddled with my sat nav to find an alternative route I considered shouting over to the canoeists to see if they would ferry me over but by the time I had come up with the idea they were strapping their canoe to the

top of their car.

A chef came out of a side door of the pub at the top of the slip road to dump a bucket of dirty water down a drain. In a last effort to follow the route I

asked him if there was any chance of crossing the river, thinking perhaps the pub had a small boat to ferry people across. He gave me the kind of look he probably normally reserved for the waiting staff and muttered, "Not without a snorkel," before retreating back into the kitchen.

My detour meant that I missed Tewkesbury with its fine abbey and, more importantly, its shops: my bottles were nearly empty. It also added a few miles but did mean I missed the first mile or so of the A38, which was not only busy but dragged up a long hill out of Tewkesbury. I was pleased to turn off onto a quieter road where the pace was so much slower.

Despite the slow pace there was an excellent sign, just before a roadside pond, politely requesting road users to show a modicum of caution and courtesy: For Ducks Sake Slow!

I entered the village of Twyning and started scanning the surrounds for a shop. The name of the village instantly put me in mind of the tea brand Twinings (which I thought was spelt Twynings) and I wondered whether it was based or founded there. I asked in the village shop (hooray!) but they had no idea. When I returned home I Googled it [I'm not sponsored by Google, though you may think so – perhaps I should talk to them...].

Despite its spelling, the name of the village is pronounced 'twinning', meaning between the rivers (Severn and Avon) in old English. Thomas Twining, the founder of Twinings tea, grew up in the village but his family moved to London in the late 17<sup>th</sup> century when he was 9 years old. He opened Britain's first known tea room at No. 216 Strand, London, in 1706. Remarkably it is still open today and is London's longest-standing rate-payer. The firm also holds the world's oldest logo, in continuous use since it was created in 1787.

It is possible that Thomas Twining was born in one of the black and white Tudor houses that the village boasts. Or he could have lived in one of a number of others that were lost to fire in years past. Local rumour is that the fire was arson, perpetrated to make room for new development.

Pedalling out of the village I turned onto a narrow lane with an 'Unsuitable for HGVs' sign. In Devon this is a sign to be feared. It can normally be translated to 'Shitty Lane' or 'Only Suitable for Goats'. However my fears were unfounded for in this part of the world it meant beautiful quiet lane.

Being on a beautiful quiet lane was fortunate: having glugged down copious quantities of liquid in Twyning I was in need of releasing some from the other end of the system. So when I came upon a giant white rabbit leaning over a fence less than a mile down the lane I stopped. He seemed friendly and had a sign upon which was writ, "What is this life, if full of care, we have no time to stop and stare..."

This is the first two

lines of the poem, Leisure, by William Henry Davies:

What is this life if, full of care,
We have no time to stand and stare.
No time to stand beneath the boughs
And stare as long as sheep or cows.
No time to see, when woods we pass,
Where squirrels hide their nuts in grass.
No time to see, in broad daylight,
Streams full of stars, like skies at night.
No time to turn at Beauty's glance,
And watch her feet, how they can dance.
No time to wait till her mouth can
Enrich that smile her eyes began.
A poor life this is if, full of care,
We have no time to stand and stare.

My older sons would find the line about the squirrels hilarious. Nevertheless, aside from hiding my nuts in the grass the poem summed up the mental approach I was trying to take for the ride so I did stop and stare. And wee.

~~Piddling~~ Pedalling around the corner I found a sign for Showborough House. I was later to discover that it is owned by the artist Andrew Roache who opens the garden for exhibits of local sculpture. The rabbit was one of his works (and I didn't wee on it, just near it, discreetly behind a bush).

A mere few hundred metres down the lane the route directed me onto a footpath. It didn't even look much like a footpath, being covered in rubble. I picked my way past the rubble and found a very wet, thin, muddy strand of path overgrown with nettles and punctuated with rocks. Aware of my pledge to follow the route (except through rivers and houses) I continued on, testing my (non-existent) off road skills to the limit in my attempt not to put a foot down. This was something I didn't want to do because the mud was getting deeper by the metre. By the time it had reached halfway up the spokes I realised I was getting into trouble: this was not a place to be on narrow tyres. I was either going to have to put a foot down up to my ankle in the mud or tumble into the nettles and brambles.

Bouncing into a particularly wet muddy section I hit an unseen obstruction under the ooze. My handlebars skewed sideways and I just managed to twist my foot out of the pedal and get it down to prevent a spill. The mud was halfway up my shin and nearly at the hubs of my wheels.

Rather than put my other foot into the gloop I scooted out of the mire as best I could. Fortunately the path soon ended but my bike was in a terrible state. The mud was an inch thick around my rims and even the spokes were fat and wobbly with gloop. Fortunately my wheel hubs had not suffered but my brake callipers and my rear gears were caked in gunk. This could have represented a disaster but the path joined a farm track which led to a road. Just before the junction there was a house with the blessed sight of a reel of hose attached visible through its open back gate.

The owner of the house was a little surprised to find me knocking on their back door but was happy enough to let me borrow the hose to blast the mud from my bike and legs.

After re-oiling the bike, wringing out my socks, making a note to re-route around the footpath and adding 'ridiculously muddy footpaths' to the list of things my pledge did not apply to, I set off again, happy for my fortunate deliverance from peril but a little concerned about the time. It was now after 13:00 and I was only about 30 miles into the day. Where had the time gone? Well, aside from the impromptu bike wash I had lost some time due to the body in the water and since then had stopped several times to stand and stare, wee, take photographs and make notes. I wasn't making notes on the paper route anymore but I was still stopping very regularly to note down points of interest. I was going to have to try and minimise the stops by doing several things at each one rather than making separate stops for each thing. So if I had an interesting thought I would have to remember it until I stopped to take a photo. And whilst stopped I should try and have a wee, take some vitamin I, transfer food from my bag to my pockets etc. I needed to be more organised.

After a few miles of choppy lanes I rolled into Worcester and onto the Worcester and Birmingham Canal. Funnily enough it links Worcester and Birmingham, starting at the Worcester end via a river lock with the Severn. 29 miles and 58 locks later it ends at Gas Street Basin in Birmingham. I was only following it to traverse Worcester, which was a shame because 30 of those locks are the Tardebigge Locks that we had climbed with our barge on our double speed circling of that two week barging loop I mentioned earlier.

In my endeavours to not make as many stops I forgot many things before committing them to paper. The trouble was I was getting very tired and my brain, fallible at the best of times, wasn't able to retain thoughts. I tried running them over and over, chant-like in my head but ended up playing Chinese whispers with myself. So my memories of the next few miles are a bit of a blur. I left the canal onto lanes for about 5 miles to climb and then descend into Droitwich Spa. 7 more miles of lanes followed, the last part of which took me through Harlebury Trading Estate, mainly through lots of no entries! I managed to find a shop not long after climbing a short but stiff hill just beyond the trading estate and then joined the A449.

The A449 was horribly busy. All my most miserable memories of the trip are of busy A roads. I think it was the clash between the capillary network of calm, quiet lanes, paths and canals and the frenetic pace and noise of the main arteries of England's roads. The route seemed to just use the two extremes, most likely because it was programmed to use all the capillaries but at times had to jump across from one branch to another and the only way was by main road due to some natural constriction point, like a gap in the hills or a river crossing. In fact it is notable at certain points that the three main transport methods of the last 300 years, canals, railways and roads, all converge cheek by jowl or even crossing over and under each other.

5 miles later I breathed a sigh of relief and my shoulders notably relaxed when I left the A449 and joined the Staffordshire and Worcestershire Canal towpath. True, it wasn't an idyllic setting, being rather urban, but there weren't any lorries trying to crush me.

Canals in urban areas tend to tour the back-sides of towns. In their heyday the waterside would have been the bustling centre but those days are long gone. They are now backwaters and often dumping grounds.

The sight of the half-submerged wrecks of 3 shopping trollies sticking out of the water at a turning point in the canal sparked across my synapses and lifted a memory. Hadn't I been here before? Surely I had turned the barge here, trying to avoid those shopping trollies [although probably not the same ones]? It had been the last voyage my wife and I had made pre-children. In fact she had been pregnant at the time so I had been doing all the steering and manoeuvring single handed, which had made turning more difficult, not having someone to fend off the circling trollies with a long pole.

I was further persuaded I had been there because alongside the turning point was surely the supermarket we had shopped at to top up our dwindling supplies. Then shortly after I was convinced. Cycling under the A456 and up the side of a lock I

popped out before the stunning view of a church that I had photographed before. This time I stopped to take a photo of someone else's barge chugging out of the lock into the basin below the church. The picturesque church, incidentally, is St Mary's. Whilst recorded in the

Domesday Book the current buildings mostly date from the 15<sup>th</sup> and 16<sup>th</sup> centuries.

On the opposite side of the canal, below the church, was a metal crane originally used to help unload heavy cargo from the commercial barges on the canal. In these days of leisure use it might still be useful for hauling water soaked corgis from the water. That might seem a bit random but I will elucidate.

Companion on all our barging holidays was our faithful Pembrokeshire Corgi, Bronwyn. She was the same as the dogs the Queen has but with an undocked tail: a magnificently bushy affair that she waved behind her like a banner. On our first barging holiday we were working our way through a series of locks when we noticed Bronwyn had disappeared, no longer getting under our feet as we tried to swing the lock gates closed. I quickly trotted back to the last lock to find her clinging to the side. Soaked and bedraggled, the side was too high and her back end with that thick bushy tail was too waterlogged for her to drag herself out. Fortunately she had a harness on so I managed to heave her out. The crane would have been useful though because the water was murky and stinky. So was the dog. And so was I after being enthusiastically thanked by said dog.

Bathing an unwilling dog is difficult at the best of

times but trying to do so in the tight confines of a narrow boat shower requires the handling powers of an octopus. Eventually though, Bronwyn and I emerged on the towpath, both still soaked but at least this time with clean water.

At the next lock I kept a close eye on Bronwyn. That was how I saw her fall in the second time. When crossing lock gates there is a narrow walkway with gaps between the gate and the bank. The gap on these locks were wider than most and when Bronwyn had tried to hop across she hadn't made it.

Re-washed, Bronwyn spent the next few locks on the barge.

The memories had me smiling and it gave me a warm glow of familiarity to know I had been to this place before. I experienced a sense of security that was most welcome after feeling so out of place on the busy highway just a few minutes before. There was nothing else for it: I would have to find out where I actually was.

My route was taking me on so many small lanes, footpaths and canals that I often passed through towns without even knowing their names. Barging is very similar, there being few town signs on the canals. Having been here twice I was determined to put a name to the place so I asked an angler perched on the canal side. He answered me in a foreign language, probably telling me he was foreign and didn't understand me. I knew how he felt so smiled and pedalled on.

Next I stopped a couple strolling along the canal towpath. They were from Kings Lynn on a barging holiday and had no idea where they were. Why is it whenever you ask for directions from anyone it always turns out they are just as lost as you?

Almost in desperation I made a third enquiry and was informed I was in Kidderminster. I assumed that was correct.

I spent another idyllic 6 miles on the canal reminiscing about barging holidays. The only down side was grating over very sad memories of Bronwyn's last barging trip. It was my 2 eldest boys' first barging trip and by that stage Bronwyn was very old, very large and mostly blind. She was affectionately known to the boys as Big Fat Slug, they not having known her in any other state. They probably couldn't imagine her leaping around and swimming about in the canal.

Bronwyn was clearly on her last days but she seemed to be enjoying the trip, being able to sit on the back with me, sniffing the sniffs as I steered the barge. In fact I think she enjoyed it so much she hung on until our last day and then passed away in the night. It was a sad

funeral procession home with all the luggage crammed in the boot and Bronwyn laid out in state in the roof box.

The sight of the prettiest bridge on any of the canals I had found so far cheered me up though. The only downside was that I had to cross it and join up with the A449 again. It

was no better that the last stretch. In fact it was now rush hour and was far worse. I endured it for 6 miles and then had to turn left, halfway up a long
drag. Normally left turns are the easiest and safest but not in this case. The path I needed to turn onto was on a bridge above my head. To get to it I was going to have to cross the road and climb the steps on the other side.

The road was so busy I had to wait 5 minutes for a gap in the traffic but it was worth it. The path, the South Stafford-shire Railway Walk, was flat and straight and had a good surface but above all it was traffic free and very quiet, once out of earshot of the A449. The walk took me about 6 miles from Wombourne to Wolverhampton where it terminated, the route then jumping straight back onto the Staffordshire and Worcestershire Canal.

Unfortunately, after 3 miles I was ejected back onto the A449. It was twilight now and I started pushing hard on the pedals, wishing to be off of the busy main road before dark. It made for a frenetic 5 miles but just before Penkridge I re-joined the Staffordshire and Worcestershire Canal tow path once more.

Why there was a need for the road section I am unsure. Perhaps the tow path disappears or is wholly unsuitable for bikes. Having said that, the next 7 miles of towpath to Stafford were not exactly suitable for a racing bike. The whole section was mud and grass and parts were fairly overgrown.

By this stage twilight was dwindling to dark and the ducks had come ashore to line the canal like sentries. As I trundled past they muttered, "Bike, bike, bike…" at me. Quite bright for ducks.

After the first mile it was totally dark and my full concentration was needed to make sure I didn't hit any unseen obstacles, such as ducks, and flip into the canal. As a consequence my speed slowed to barely walking pace. It took me an hour to cover the last 6 miles!

By the time the canal path spat me out at Stafford I was very tired and quite sore. Strangely the sorest part was my face: I had been grinning like a manic for the last hour, thoroughly enjoying my night time jaunt along the canal. It was then that I dubbed my trip, 'Roy's Mad Adventure'. Compared to what some people get up to it wasn't very mad at all but it's a matter of perspective. As I trundled the last few hundred metres down the road to the B&B I decided to treat the rest of the ride very much in the pioneering spirit.

Safely installed at my B&B and freshly showered I discovered there was no heating and the window did not open. Having trod the grapes on my kit to wash it I had to put it back on damp and use body heat to dry it. It wasn't particularly pleasant but I consoled myself that real pioneers probably had to deal with rather more dangerous perils and hardships.

Whilst munching my staple Pot Noodle from the day's Red Cross parcel I noted down the statistics from my sat nav. Notable was the extra 10 miles or so due to my early detours caused by bodies in the water. I can't hold that against the poor soul though. Equally worthy of note was the mere 827 metres of ascent. I do not think I have ever ridden over 100 miles with so little climbing! Not that it had helped my speed: average moving speed 11.7 mph but average including stops below 9mph. I think this was largely due to the type of track I was cycling on and the constant stopping and starting to bypass cycling obstructions. Pragmatically I had to admit that the tired legs might also have had something to do with it.

As I contemplated the day's ride the main thing that stuck in my mind was the stark contrast between the tranquillity of the canal and the frenetic energy of the main roads. I had spent some hours reminiscing about canal holidays and sadly departed doggy friends and other hours sweating in wild eyed panic. Surely, I thought, there must be a way to avoid the main roads or at least minimise them. When I returned home I would take a closer look at the route and find a safer, more pleasant way.

| Distance: | 109 miles | Av speed: | 11.7 mph |
|---|---|---|---|
| Time cycling: | 9:16 | Time overall: | 12:17 |
| Av heart rate: | 127 bpm | Calories burnt: | 3,834 |
| Total ascent: | 827 m | Max speed: | 28.2 mph |

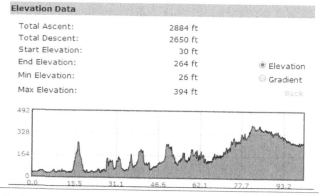

| Elevation Data | | |
|---|---|---|
| Total Ascent: | 2884 ft | |
| Total Descent: | 2650 ft | |
| Start Elevation: | 30 ft | |
| End Elevation: | 264 ft | ◉ Elevation |
| Min Elevation: | 26 ft | ◯ Gradient |
| Max Elevation: | 394 ft | Back |

# Chapter Nine

## Day 4 – Every Day is a Good Day on the Canal

7:00am was too early for breakfast. At home I normally only eat breakfast a couple of hours, at least, after waking. I wasn't intending to get up at 5:00am so after rolling out of bed into my cycling kit I didn't feel that set for eating.

Sat contemplating the menu I decided it was time to start taking on some caffeine; it might invigorate my mind and my appetite.

Sipping coffee I contemplated the day ahead. As far as I could remember I would be skirting around Manchester and going through Preston to finish in Condor Green, a few miles south of Lancaster. I couldn't remember exactly how much but thought there was a fair bit of canal tow path involved.

The problem was, I had studied the route at the microscopic detail level - to see what path surfaces were like, what was at different junctions and how busy the roads were - but had no real concept of where I was actually travelling, other than generally northwards. I had looked so closely that I had been focused on the leaves and hadn't even seen the trees, let alone the wood. However, I did know that by the end of the day I would be halfway. In fact, in terms of miles I would be a little over halfway.

Although the caffeine was starting to kick in I still

couldn't face a Full English so decided on egg and bacon, forgoing the sausage, tomato and mushrooms.

By 07:45am I had eaten, packed and was sat astride the bike ready for the off. A quick text to show I was still around and I was away.

Some days, rarely, you set off on your bike and feel great. Your legs are strong, there are no pains in your shoulders or back, your energy levels are high and you are actively buzzing with the prospect of the ride ahead. Today was not one of those days. Still, not surprising really with 3 days and 370 miles of road (and canal path and disused railway and gnarly footpath) under my tyres.

On the positive, my knee was holding out and my shoulders and butt were faring well. I think that was down to the 'don't push on the pedals' policy I was adopting. That may sound a little bizarre. Of course, I was pushing on the pedals. But not so as to be considered too much effort: I had to conserve my energy to complete each day fresh enough to want to start the next day. My knee was also a concern and I didn't want it to turn into an excuse – again. And if I wasn't going to allow myself to use it as an excuse then I had better make sure it didn't hurt. I didn't want to have to do the manly thing of struggling on in pain; I rather struggle on without pain, thank you very much.

Willing my heavy legs to rotate around the cranks as I crept though the back alleys of Stafford, I felt sure I would soon hit that zone were no matter how heavy the legs feel they still seem to spin around, maintaining a steady, if not fast, pace for mile after mile. That was the hope.

The back alleys took me to the Astonfields Balancing Lakes. The name immediately conjured in my mind a Dr

Seuss type image of lakes tottering around on stilts but the reality was more mundane. The lakes were created, one in the 1970s and the other in the 1990s, to help maintain an even, balanced flow of the Marston Brook thus reducing the risk of flood. The bird life promised on the information sign was not much in evidence as the sun managed to drag itself high enough in the sky to peak between the trees but it made a nice peaceful interlude before hitting the A513 on the outskirts of Stafford.

Fortunately, it was still too early for the road to be busy. In any event, after a mile I turned off onto a narrower way to cut across to the A34. Despite the hour this was a busy dual carriageway. Rather than tackle the carriageway itself I joined the cycle path on the pavement, contra flowing the road for a mile before connecting via lane to my first canal of the day.

The Trent and Mersey canal was one of the first canals built in Staffordshire, work starting in 1766. Many local landowners and merchants contributed to the project, including Josiah Wedgwood who ensured that the canal ran past the new factory he was building in Stoke-on-Trent. No doubt he recognised the advantages that canals offered by way of transporting goods in bulk and, most importantly for a fine china producer, smoothly.

Each canal has different ways of dealing with bridges and locks and the Trent and Mersey favoured a cobbled surface. It didn't particularly favour me but at least it gave my legs an early morning massage.

At bridge 100 (pictured) the tow path crosses from one side of the canal to the other, over the bridge. The exit from the bridge is a very steep and sharp 270 degree turn, all on cobbles! With narrow wheels I was very conscious that one false move would have my

front tyre wedged and me face planting the cobbles.

Before each bridge along the canal was a 'low headroom' sign. This was very sensible for there was little room under the bridges. What is a mystery is why the signs were at the top posts that were taller than the bridge in question. Maybe they were trying to warn cyclists riding Penny Farthings? Or birds?

I followed the canal for 10 miles to - and through - Stoke-on-Trent, spotting the new Wedgwood factory set back on the right a little before the town. No doubt I also passed the site of the original factory but I had little time to ponder its location having been ejected onto the manically busy A53.

I decided to stick to the pavement/cycleway where I could. I lost a lot of time at roundabouts, waiting for gaps in the endless streams of traffic at each artery

I had to cross, but better late than a smear across the tarmac, as they say.

I was pleased to turn off onto a path through Whitfield Valley Nature Reserve. The path had dealt with the problem of slowing cyclists in an ingenious way. Though hard to describe I would have labelled the obstacles as shoulder compression gates. Basically there were two inverted U shaped poles with a metal plate on each held parallel to one another at shoulder height and a little over shoulder width apart. This meant that whilst cyclists had to slow to an almost stop they could remain in the saddle, bumping shoulders with the metal plates. I later found a similar gate and took a photo, which is probably a lot clearer than my description.

The paths were generally in good condition for cyclists and the route boasted an impressive bridge, reflecting a considerable amount of investment. Some sections were not tarmacked though. I was riding in the dry but things might have been stickier if I had been riding in summer, when it tends to rain a lot more.

According to its sign the reserve boasts a wide range of wildlife, including skylark, grey partridge, barn owls, kestrels and water voles. All I managed to catch sight of was a fat tabby cat. Maybe he was a prodigious hunter.

The track crosses or passes under several roads and transforms into the Biddulph Valley Way after about 5 miles. I stopped by the sign to text home and make a few notes. It was 10:41 and I was 30 miles into the day, so an average of 10mph.

The Biddulph Valley Way is a leisure walk/cycle path utilising another disused railway. The Biddulph Valley Railway opened in 1859 and was used predominantly for freight – coal from North Staffordshire to Congleton and sand, Congleton's speciality export, on the return trip for the potteries.

A passenger service operated for 60 years but closed in 1927. The freight continued until 1968 when it fell to the Beeching Axe.

I always feel a bit sorry for Dr Beeching. Sure, with  hindsight his reforms were perhaps too broad and the axe fell too swiftly and without proper public consultation but at the time British Rail was losing £140 million a year, a lot more money then than now. The network was too intricate with many branch lines carrying insufficient traffic. The thing is, I like trains and can romanticise about how great it would be to still have all those lines open: the places we could visit and the access it would provide for locals. But the reality is I have a car and it is a darn sight easier to use that. Apart from getting from Plymouth to Penzance at the beginning of my trip I hadn't been on a non-leisure or tube train for years.

Anyway, without Beeching I would now be stuck on the A527 rather than this tranquil cycleway. It is not what happens that matters, it is how you deal with the consequences. Well done Cheshire East Council and Staffordshire County Council for creating and maintaining the path.

Just after the end of the track I found a shop and was grateful to fill my bottles. Even though I would be travelling through some very urban areas I couldn't be sure when I would next see a shop.

On the lanes that followed I took a photo that I thought of as 'fifty shades of hay bales'. The latest farmer based technology must be a bailer that plastic seals the hay in the field. I have been noticing more and more of these black lumps in the fields. For the farmer it is obviously a great convenience but one of my favourite rural scenes on a sunny day is a stubble field dotted with bright yellow cotton reels of hay.

Coal black cotton reels do not really do it for me. Given a choice between wind farms and black cotton reels I would choose wind farms.

A few miles later I found myself back on the A34, which would take me 9 miles to Wilmslow. The first 6 miles were fairly hectic but after a fairly new looking roundabout there was a separate cycleway.

I stopped to text home, to show signs of life, and noticed my sat nav was showing 66.6 km (I use km because Audax rides are all routed in km). I texted that I hoped it wasn't a bad omen (excuse the pun).

It turns out that it was. I misread the route and ended up on a parallel road, which ended abruptly at someone's private mansion. Rather than backtrack I followed a footpath towards the A34. It was very overgrown so I had to go by foot. Then the path just ended at a ditch. There was no option but to climb into it and clamber back out the other side with my bike. Then I was

forced to scramble up and down a large bank on the side of the A34 to regain the cycle path. It gave me a very practical demonstration as to why simple ditch and bank defences were so effective. Although most attackers wouldn't have been carrying a loaded push bike.

The cycle path

had a slightly downward gradient so I whizzed into Wilmslow where I stopped by St Bartholomew's Church to eat something and text home again. The church had caught my eye because there were genuine gargoyles leering down at me from its tower. They could have done with a bit of a clean though; they and the buff sandstone of the church had been blackened by the traffic fumes from the adjacent road. But then the building has been there a while: the current building dates mostly from the early 16th century but there is documentary evidence of a church on the site as early as 1246.

The clock on the tower showed it was 12:25. I was 45 miles in and had been on the road for 4:40 hours so I was averaging just under 10 mph. I thought perhaps it was time to roll on and try to get the average on the other side of 10.

Leaving the church I climbed the appropriately named Cliff Road. It probably wasn't that steep but after two days of virtually constant flat it was a bit of a shock. Things weren't helped by a repeat performance a couple of hundred metres later. A third ramp raised me to Styal Prison where the sign on the downward carriageway warned of 12%. So, nothing like the 20% hills in Devon and Cornwall but they felt just as bad.

I continued on the B5166 into the outskirts of Manchester where I crossed the A5103 on a footbridge and turned under the M60 and into Kenworthy Woods.

Running along the Mersey River valley this area was originally farmland, subject to frequent flooding. Later gravel was extracted from the land and subsequently it was used as a landfill site,

predominantly for bombing debris after the Manchester bombing raids in the Second World War. This history is not evident now though, at least not on the surface. The landfill was capped with topsoil in the 1970s and the first woodland was planted. In 1997 the co-op funded a scheme to plant 32 acres of native trees. Now the woodlands feel mature yet fresh and are a haven for birdlife (no fat tabby here).

With all of this beauty around me I chose to take a photo of my shadow, presumably to prove that the sun did occasionally shine on this ride.

I exited the woods cycling alongside a massive graveyard and then under a railway and the Bridgewater canal to sharp turn onto the canal towpath.

The very first building on the canal was the Watch

House Cruising Club. I was amused to see a sign stating that cyclists were welcome and another stating that no dogs were allowed. It is a rare establishment that ranks cyclists above dogs these days.

I learnt from an information sign that the Watch House was originally a staging post for passenger boats that ran along the canal before the railways. Staff would wait with fresh horses so that the horses could be changed without stopping the boat. As I was discovering myself, if you are travelling at a plod you need to minimise the number of stops (I reminded myself as I climbed back onto the saddle).

The same sign declared the Bridgewater Canal was, "...one of the most important in the world and its status is beginning to be recognised." Having opened in 1761 it is obviously a slow burner.

Less than a mile along the canal path, in Stretford, I came upon a sign stating that the towpath was closed and I was diverted up some steps to the very busy A56 heading into Manchester (and out of Manchester I suppose). The road was dual carriageway with four lanes to each carriage at this point. Fortunately I didn't

have to cycle along it, just cross it and descend steps the other side back to the towpath. What would have taken 20 seconds on the towpath stretched out to over 5 minutes of waiting for two sets of poorly synched traffic lights. It made me appreciate how easily I was slipping through these urban areas on the flat, snaky canals.

I tried to make the most of the towpath whilst I had it and started to actually push against the pedals a little. It didn't do me any good: after a mile or so I was hitting the brakes having caught sight of the Taj Mahal out of the corner of my eye. Wheeling back I was disappointed to discover it wasn't the Taj Mahal after all. It was the Barton Square Shopping Centre. Perhaps a teeny bit pretentious?

I stopped some time later to take a picture of a far more eye pleasing building, probably the grandest I had seen on any of the canals. In its day it would have been just as pretentious but now was a thing of beauty.

Occasionally the canals throws in obstacles to make cyclists dismount, usually if there is a particularly blind or low bridge to go under. One canal had gates installed on the towpath that were helpfully spring loaded so you didn't have to worry about closing them. The only problem was that they were so spring loaded that if you hesitated for a moment they slammed into your rear wheel, thrusting you either along the track or off the bike. No doubt the designers had been inspired by the motivator from the Big Red Balls obstacle on the Wipe Out television programme.

Following the Bridgewater canal for 13 miles I discovered it was much keener than other canals to make cyclists dismount to go under bridges. A number of different tricks had been used. It tried the compression gates but they were so narrow they were more like constriction gates, forcing you to dismount, unless you had the handling skills to rotate your upper body 90 degrees without altering course by a centimetre. I was too weary to try. It also utilised lines of raised bricks. It would have been possible to bunny hop these but I didn't fancy failing and ending up in the canal. A similar technique employed was a rail right across the path a few inches high, easy to step over but not so easy to bunny hop. Even a pro would have struggled with several kilos of bag on the back.

However, the simplest trick used to persuade you

to dismount and walk was to make the towpath extremely muddy. Having not rained for a day or two the mud was mostly dry but extremely rutted with tyre tracks. The effect was not unlike cycling over corrugated iron, just not as regular in its pattern of bumps and grooves.

There is a famous cycling race in the spring called Paris-Roubaix. It is about 160 miles long, which is a considerable distance to ride let alone race over, but to add to the difficulty the route takes in a number of sections of ancient cobbled farm track totalling 30 miles in all. Apparently the secret to riding the cobbles is to hit them as fast as possible and kind of skip over them, like a flat stone skimming over water. The trick is to keep the momentum up or, like the stone, you will plunge to the depths.

I hit the rutted mud hard and kept the pressure on the pedals. As I skipped over the ruts I noted the tyre tracks were all from wide tyres with knobbly treads, not narrow road bike tyres. Well sod it: I might have had to stop for rails and bricks and constriction gates but I wasn't going to stop for mud!

About a mile into the 'cobbles' I met a fellow biker coming the other way. He had a full suspension mountain bike. He was walking. He looked at me askance and queried what my butt was made of. "Feels like fire!" I shouted over my shoulder as I rattled by. You see, the other trick to riding the cobbles is not to get out of the saddle because the back end jerks around too much. You're telling me!

To leave the canal I had to dismount again to climb over a footbridge crossing the canal. I have to admit that I was quite relieved to get out of the saddle and peel the seat pad from my butt.

The route led me through a park and down a residential street to a small grassy area with a wooden rail fence, beyond which was barren scrubland. The sat nav route pointed, rather hopefully, towards it. There was no path visible, not even evidence of walkers crossing the grass.

I zoomed out on the map and saw the route crossed a lot of white space before it came to a road again. Oh well, plod on!

Wheeling the bike over the grass I found a step over break in the fence where I could haul the bike over. On the other side the path was more obvious but it was still just a thin strip of mud worming through the long grass and brambles. I rode up a slight rise to find the path suddenly widened considerably at the top, plenty of room for two cyclists to pass each other. Why this wasn't continued down to the road is a mystery, at least to me.

I was quickly into a whole network of paths and had to concentrate to keep on my sat nav route. I might have become a bit anal about it because at one point I found myself forcing a path through bushes in an attempt to keep on track.

Some parts of the path were very muddy. The area must have had more rain recently than the canal. Or perhaps the high clay content of the mud made it less porous, so it didn't drain well. It certainly made it particularly sticky and, despite my earlier vow not to stop for mud, I had to do so three times to clear the space (very little) between my front tyre and the forks on the frame. This is one of the areas in which a road bike is just not designed for off road routes. The geometry of the frame is all wrong, the centre of gravity is too high, there is no suspension and the wheels are too narrow. It results in a very bumpy and skiddy ride. I made a note that this part of the route should be avoided on a road bike, at least if it had rained in the last few days.

I was quite relieved to reach a stretch of road. So relieved I stopped to call home, needing to hear a friendly voice. I had seen hardly a soul all day yet I kept hearing kids in the distance. Probably emanating from some school playground a few hundred metres away but it served to remind me that I was all alone and missing my family.

Following my 'do many things at each stop' routine I also wee'd and took a photo. Not of weeing: of birds up on the wires and the telegraph poles, as the Dire Straits lyric has it. It was a sight I hadn't seen for a long time, now that most cables run underground. In fact it put me in mind of musical notation. Not being able to read music I had no idea of the tune but it looked very brash, overly busy and discordant.

It was now 15:26, so 7:40 hours in and 73 miles covered. So my big push to tip the average over 10 mph was not a success: I was still averaging a little under 10 mph. With 37 miles to go I calculated I would reach my B&B around 19:30.

The road didn't last long. I followed another very off road track around the back of Hindley Prison (who knew there were so many prisons dotted about the place?) and then I joined the Wigan Greenheart Cycleway. As part

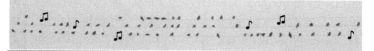

of a maintained cycleway this part of the route had a much better surface but considering the title 'cycleway' they had some bizarre anti-cycle obstacles. At one point, on a completely straight section with clear view for a couple of hundred metres either way, there was an obstacle requiring you to lift your bike over it. I have no objection to this at danger points, especially when paths are shared with pedestrians but why here? It can't have been cheap to install.

The path took me onto the Leeds and Liverpool Canal, which wends its way for 127 miles between the two towns including 91 locks, which makes it the longest in Northern England. Not having to worry so much about contouring, the M62 does it in 74 miles (without any locks).

Work started on the canal in 1770 but it was only completed in 1816, some 46 years later. With its junction to the Aire & Calder Navigation at Leeds it provides a waterway navigation across the country from the North Sea to the Irish Sea. Amazingly the canal was still in commercial use for portage of large tonnages of coal into the 1950s, traffic only ending when canal side collieries closed with the introduction of natural gas.

About 4 miles along the canal I entered Lancashire by crossing over the River Douglas on an aqueduct, just south of Adlington. The sign was pot marked where locals had used it for target practice. A continuation of the War of the Roses? Wrong border for that.

Some sections of the canal were riddled with

ridges of dried mud, making them the bumpiest I had encountered. If it had been very wet it might have been impassable on a road bike. It was fortunate that I wasn't cycling the whole 127 miles of the canal but I did still have another 6 miles before I would turn off. To compensate I was blessed with a strong tailwind. When I had my Rainlegs on they acted like a sail, catching the wind and skimming me over the bumps Paris-Roubaix style.

On the downside I hadn't seen a shop for hours. Both my bottles were dry. Cycling by the canal wasn't helping: "Water, water everywhere, Nor any drop to drink," as Colridge put it in The Rime of the Ancient Mariner. Of course he was talking about salt water and I could probably drink from the canal and live to tell the tale. But I wasn't that desperate. Yet.

Like an ever optimistic dog that keeps flipping its empty food bowl over in the hopes of finding more underneath, I lifted my bottle to my lips for the third time. It was still empty. Try again in a minute.

Not long before turning off the canal I overheard a snippet of conversation between an angler and a bargeman as he chugged slowly past. He asked the angler if it had been a good day and the response was, "Every day is a good day on the canal."

When I finally left the canal just south of Whittle-le-Woods it was a bitter sweet moment. I had to agree with the angler: I had enjoyed the canals the most on the trip and it was a real shame that they were over. Whilst the condition of the tow paths had become steadily worse the further north I had travelled, I would dearly miss them. Then again, as my tyres hissed across the silky smooth tarmac, my butt heaved a sigh of relief (not a euphemism).

In Whittle-le-Woods the Bay Horse public house beckoned and the bar lady were gracious enough to fill my bottles. There was an elderly couple (although I doubt they would thank me for the description) sat outside enjoying their drinks in the chilling wind. They proceeded to chat to me and I got steadily colder, my sweat dampened lycra and heavily ventilated helmet providing considerably less insulation than their thick jackets and woolly hats. I tried making some pointed comments about how far I had to go and the fact that the light was already beginning to fade. This just led to a conversation about where I had cycled from, which led onto the fact that I was cycling LEJOG. I was starting to shiver as this sparked a story about their mate who had cycled LEJOG in a day and a half, "…and that was in the good old days when there were proper bikes, not all this foreign rubbish." I knew this was nonsense because the record is 1 day 20 hours 4 minutes 20 seconds (although it has been completed in 1 day 17 hours, 4 minutes and 22 seconds on a recumbent cycle). I kept my cool though, in fact I was bloody frozen, and refrained from contradicting them. As they rambled on (they were a great double act, finishing off each other's sentences) they started talking about Hogs and Harleys and it dawned on me that their mate must have had done it on a motorbike! A day and a half? The bloke on the recumbent had almost managed that!

I excused myself and pedalled off at speed in an attempt to warm up.

The Cuerden Valley Park Cycle Route led me to Bamber Bridge, the last section being on a footbridge over the M6. Seeing the rush of traffic below put the

few bumps on the canal into perspective.

An old tramway then took me into Preston and after a couple of back roads I was on the A6 ring way. It was mad up to the right hand turn, especially because I had to move over a couple of lanes to be in the right position at the lights. As the lights changed to green I prayed I wouldn't fumble the cleat insertion into the pedal. My heart was already racing and I didn't need a load of car horns whipping it faster. Thankfully my foot snicked onto place and with a couple of thrusts I was across the junction and hugging the left hand kerb.

The road was busy but quietened down as Preston was left behind. Before long a cycle lane appeared and with the assistance of a massive tailwind I soared along the road. It was gently undulating but with the added thrust of the wind I was able to zip down the downs and maintain speed on the ups. If I had thought to unfurl my Rainlegs I might have taken off!

Despite the added speed it was still nearly dark when I rolled in the B&B. Although calling it a B&B is a bit of an understatement, it was a Heritage Inn and far plusher than anything I had stayed in so far on the trip.

To celebrate reaching the halfway point I splashed out on a steak dinner and a pint of Guinness (good for the blood).  Because I was riding for charity they gave me a discount but it was still £20.  Now that isn't a vast sum but up until that point, including day zero, my total spend had been less than £10, thanks to my Red Cross parcels and parsimonious ways.

As I sat waiting for the steak to arrive I texted home saying I was thinking of writing a scientific paper on the diversity of canal towpath surfaces and their relative destructive effect on bikes and their riders.  Surfaces would include: tarmac (with and without tree roots erupting from the surface several cm upward), cinder, gravel (light or deep), mud (dried to a furrowed, corrugated surface or thickly wet), cobbles, grass and just plain stones.  Or of course there is the straight forward 3 inch wide mud strip worn several inches down into the grass (with or without brambles and stinging nettles either side) requiring precision cycling to avoid hitting the edge and being tipped into the murky depths of the canal.

I was enjoying the view of the floodlit lock by the side of the restaurant, the ideal setting after my day on the canals, when a reply to my text came in.  Appropriate to the setting, my text alert is a recording of my youngest son singing, "Row, row, row your boat, gently down the stream..."  However when it was recorded he was only two and whilst he had the tune sorted he didn't know the words.  He did have older brothers to teach him though so it came out as, "Poo, poo, Poo poo poo, Poo poo poo Poo Poo..." (sing along now).  My phone was set on its loudest setting, to give me some chance of hearing it whilst cycling, and once the alert starts it cannot be stopped.  It just kept getting louder and louder until the entire restaurant was treated to the 'poo poo song' from the table with the lout dressed in slightly ripe lycra. It did raise some smiles amongst the frowns though.

Fortunately my steak arrived so I could focus on that. It looked up at me and said, "I am too big for you. You will never eat all of me!" It stood no chance. Five minutes later it was demolished and I was heading upstairs for a shower and a Pot Noodle.

Noting down my stats for the day I totted up the total distance travelled so far: 482 miles. More than halfway but still less than I managed on my failed LEL. I had gone a lot further on my dodgy knee than I thought!

| Distance: | 112 miles | Av speed: | 13.7 mph |
|---|---|---|---|
| Time cycling: | 8:37 | Time overall: | 12:02 |
| Av heart rate: | 128 bpm | Calories burnt: | 3,842 |
| Total ascent: | 827 m | Max speed: | 30.4 mph |

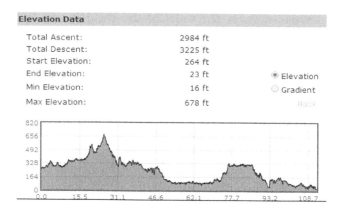

# Chapter Ten

## Day 5 – Rain dampens the earth and the minds of men

It rained in the night.

It was still raining in the morning.

I plodded down to breakfast. Helping myself to muesli I sat and perused the menu. I couldn't get inspired. Slowly masticating (that's chewing, if you're reading fast) my way through the muesli I watched the rain drops chase each other down the windows. The lock outside didn't look so appealing in the rain.

I studied the menu again. Five breakfasts into the ride I couldn't summon the willpower to face a Full English. I plumped for a bacon omelette.

The rain was beating against the windows now. The forecast for the next three days looked pretty gloomy; a blue tide rising northward across the map. Being particularly British about it I decided it was because my holiday was officially starting today [I work part-time, Wednesday to Friday, and it was Wednesday]. It always bloody rains on my holidays. And most Wednesday to Fridays during the hours of 07:00 – 08:00 and 16:30 –17:30, when I am cycling between work and home.

My omelette arrived. It looked excellent. It was perfectly cooked, light and fluffy. I struggled to defeat it, each bite taking an act of will, telling myself I needed to eat to move. It was a pathetic performance, a far cry from my rampaging slaughter of the steak the night before.

Finally, triumphant but not jubilant, I took the lift (fancy!) up to my room (not direct to my room: it wasn't *that* fancy). I donned my rain jacket and Rainlegs, grabbed my bag and then descended to the basement, where my bike was stored in the laundry.

Wheeling the bike out into the courtyard I was pleased to see that the rain had eased, if not stopped. Even so, this was the first day I had to start in the rain. I hate starting a ride in the rain. I don't mind it raining a minute after the start – although I would rather it didn't – but not at the start thanks.

I pedalled away at 08:02, trying to think positively: I was halfway and today I would be crossing the border into Scotland. It may seem strange to be entering Scotland on my fifth day out of eight but the reality is, Scotland is much bigger than most people appreciate. In fact the Scottish part of my journey was approximately 380 miles of the total 930 mile trip, over 40% of the distance. If you were to cycle from Southampton on the south coast of England to John O'Groats, the English section (412 miles) and the Scottish section (380 miles) are virtually the same.

So why do most people perceive Scotland as smaller than it is? My theory is the weather. Or rather the weather forecast. Weather maps show the country tilted, as if on a globe. The much more important south of the country fills most of the screen with the tiny nodule of unimportant Scotland diminished into insignificance at the top.

It's either that or people in the south just haven't given it much thought. Perhaps they should all go on a long cycle ride in the rain with nothing much else to do.

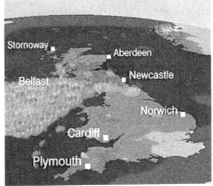

I was on the road for all of a couple of hundred metres before turning off onto the Lune Estuary cycle path. This tarmac way led me to Lancaster. It was flat, smooth and fast. At least, the latter would have been true if my legs had been working properly. They felt wooden, if wood can feel dull pain with every pedal stroke. I found a lower gear and spun along at a slightly higher cadence if no higher speed. It was a good thing the first few miles were flat, not uphill.

Rapid progress was also curtailed by the need to wee. I had only been going for a few minutes and already I felt an urgency. Although not mentioned until now, this had been an increasing problem as the days progressed. I wasn't drinking copious amounts, mainly because I only seemed to be finding shops every 40 miles or so, and yet my bladder was constantly sending messages to my brain to stop. Or rather; to go. I had been putting it down to the vibration from the canal paths but so far today things had been silky smooth. It nagged at the back of my mind that the problem was caused by the women specific vitamin pills I was taking every day. Knowing I would be taxing my system I had grabbed them from the cupboard just before I left, there being no manly vitamins available. I'm not a great believer

**125**

in artificial vitamin supplements but felt they couldn't do any harm. Now I wasn't so sure. Needing to wee every five minutes I was concerned my women's vitamins were turning me into a woman.

The cycle path kept by the River Lune in Lancaster until climbing up a bank to join the Lancaster canal. This was a double pleasant surprise. Firstly, I had thought my canal days were over and now maybe there was a last hoorah to enjoy. Secondly, the canal passed over the River Lune on a broad aqueduct.

The Lune Aqueduct was designed by civil engineer John Rennie and constructed by architect Alexander Stevens (died 1796, aged 66). Well, that's what the plaque informed me. It also stated that it was completed in 1797, a year after Alexander Stevens's death, so I guess he didn't actually do the constructing himself. It always annoys me that great civil engineering achievements are referred to as being 'constructed by' or 'completed by' the chief engineer or architect. True, without them the engineering marvel wouldn't be there but they never did the graft. What about some mention of the multitude of navvies that were the grease that enabled the industrial revolution machine to keep moving? Mutter, mutter, moan, moan, gripe, bloody rain...

Having said that, you also needed the people who put up the money. The cost of the construction was close to £50,000, equivalent to approximately £4 million now. Although working out equivalent costs is always a bit of a guestimate it is probably fairly accurate when compared with the £2.4 million cost of restoring the aqueduct in 2011.

In fact the cost was so high that another planned aqueduct at Preston was never built, leaving the Lancaster Canal short of its intended terminus. It was built to link the limestone quarries in Lancaster and Kendal with coalfields near Wigan. Black coal and white limestone were the canal's main cargoes, which is why it came to be known as the Black & White Canal.

As I cycled along the canal, the rain came and went and came again and my rain jacket was off and on and off again like a gigolo's trousers. Not being a pro (cyclist) I needed to stop for each change which was making for slow progress. To counter the problem I kept my spinnaker-like Rainlegs on to catch the still strong tailwind.

Despite having cycled 500 miles, a large proportion of which had been on designated cycle ways or roads forming part of the National Cycle Network, I had not come across many other cyclists. Of those that I had, nearly all of them were wearing helmets. [Don't worry, I'm not going to bleat on about wearing helmets, although I know I've managed to crack my own into the tarmac pretty hard on more than one occasion.] However, the head protection of choice in Lancashire seemed to be the woolly hat. They came in various colours and patterns but the same pudding basin design. Certainly no pompoms.

Passing my 4th or 5th woolly hat I pondered whether the locals knew something. Perhaps the sheep in Lancashire produced particularly tough wool, capable of bouncing off tarmac whilst cushioning the skull. Certainly they couldn't have been wearing them because of the cold, the temperature was not that low. I'm a southern softy and I was riding in shorts and a short sleeves (when not in rain gear). I stopped to make a note to look it up when I got home.

That well known student resource and provider of totally reliable information, Wikipedia, listed the Lonk sheep as a native of Lancashire, being bred there for over 200 years. The breed derives its name from the Lancashire work 'lanky', meaning long and thin. And it appears that their wool *is* known for being particularly tough and has traditionally been used to make carpet. '...and is now used in the manufacture of woolly cycle helmets,' I was tempted to add.

Another peculiarity of the Lancaster Canal was that my virtual bell stopped working. Not having a bell I had been warning pedestrians of my approach with a hail of, "Ding, ding." As I trundled by I would smooth any frowns with an explanation that it was my make shift bell. This invariably raised a smile or a chuckle but not so on the Lancaster Canal. Here it was scowls and grunts. Still, that was better than fists and curses. I put it down to the rain.

Before setting out on my journey I had selected my lightest book from the bookcase as reading material: an Ellis Peters, Cadfael novel; a medieval whodunit. I had noted down a quote from the book whilst on the train to Penzance which seemed particularly appropriate that morning: 'The rain, though welcome to the earth was disturbing and depressing to the mind of man.'

After my bonus 7 miles on the canal I bid it a final farewell and turned onto the A6. I wasn't much looking forward to it but fortunately the main traffic through the area is carried by the M6 and as a result it was much quieter than I had expected.

As I passed into Cumbria I stopped to put my rain jacket back on. I wasn't taking any chances. A few years ago, pre-children, my wife and I had taken a two week, two destination holiday. The first week was in Cumbria and the second in Spean Bridge, a few miles north of Fort William in Scotland. It had rained almost continually for the whole 14 days.

On our first day, in defiance of the conditions, we hiked up the nearest hill to take in the view of the low lying cloud. The rain was beating down so hard, Boney, our Scottie, was running around in circles trying to keep her ears from being pounded by the huge drops. By the time we returned to our holiday cottage she was soaked to the skin, much to the amusement of Bronwyn with her much thicker Corgi coat.

That afternoon we headed to the closest outdoor gear shop. We were tempted by their doggy life jackets but thought the locals might think we were taking the piss so settled for buying doggy raincoats, much to the amusement of Boney, who thought Bronwyn looked a right knob in hers. That holiday was the only time they were ever needed.

Just before 10:00 I passed a sign for the Heron Theatre. I wasn't concentrating fully, struggling as I was to work out that if I had been cycling for two hours and had covered just under 20 miles I must be averaging a little under 10 mph (I re-iterate that I was tired and my brain was not firing on both cylinders). In the background my other brain cell was wondering what sort of acts herons put on. Still double checking my maths I glimpsed a sign for the Heron Water Mill. These herons are busy thought brain cell two. It was only when my first brain cell was satisfied that 20 divided by 2 was indeed 10 that it interjected and pointed out that I might just be cycling through somewhere called Heron.

It turns out I was actually cycling through Beetham and I have no idea why herons are so prominent in the place names. Unless these places really are run by herons?

I could have followed the A6 all the way through Kendal, over Shap Fell and into Penrith but in Milnthorpe, Google headed me onto the lanes for the 8 or so miles into Kendal.

There was a high quality butcher in Milnthorpe. I know they were high quality because they had a big green canopy with 'High Quality Butchers' emblazoned across it in gold letters. I wondered if other butchers, who don't quite make the grade, have 'Average Quality Butchers' outside. Still, perhaps they had certificates inside to back up their claims. I don't know because I didn't stop. I was turning the corner and starting to climb a nasty hill, wondering why Google had taken me off the much flatter A6.

The ups and downs continued and I assumed Google had turned me into some hills to make up for the very flat last few days. Or maybe it was to wake my legs up before facing the climb up Shap Fell, between Kendal and Penrith. It was a bit of a rude wakeup call though. One hill was 15% and I stopped near the top to take a picture of some sheep kneeling down to eat the grass. It is an age old joke but in this case even the tree in the background seemed to be lying down under the strain.

As the hills continued I began to wonder if, in some bizarre mix up at the B&B, I had put the wrong legs on. The pair I was wearing seemed to belong to someone much older. I stopped to check the label: size medium, age 46. No, they were the right pair, just more worn and torn than they were a few days ago.

The last couple of miles into Kendal were downhill and I was routed through the outskirts of the town on a footpath, avoiding the traffic, and onto the A6 on the other side. Fortunately there was a shop at the junction and I topped up my drinks knowing that I was unlikely to see another shop until Penrith, another 27 miles along the road. At this stage I had been cycling for 3 hours and had covered 29.5 miles: an average speed of a smidge under 10mph. If that average continued it would be almost another 3 hours until Penrith.

If you read any accounts of cycling from Land's End to John O'Groats, the three hills most commonly mentioned are Shap Fell, Helmsdale and Berriedale Braes, the last two being within a few miles of each other on the A9 in Northern Scotland. To be honest, none of these hills are lethal if approached with the right mental attitude, although if going south to north the duo in Scotland are ready to trip up tired legs. [As an addendum to this comment I should add that I have only ridden these hills with a single bag weighing a few kilos. Being fully laden with camping gear would make them an entirely different prospect.]

Having ridden over Shap Fell on my JOGLE a few years previously I remembered it as being a long, long drag rather than a particularly arduous climb. However, on that trip I had originally planned to ride over the 25% gradient Kirkstone Pass but detoured over Shap because I was suffering from sciatica, so it might have just felt easier in comparison.

I did recall that when descending from Shap Fell I had felt glad I had climbed it from the north because the southern approach had looked quite a bit steeper, especially right near the top. So it was with a little trepidation that I left Kendal, especially with legs that didn't seem to be working too well.

After about two and a half miles of steady climbing Google turned me from the A6 and onto a

20% hill with gravel and grass in the middle: a real
Audax style lane. Despite the grind I couldn't help
but smile at the sign halfway up which suggested the
lane was liable to flooding! If it rained heavily I
would have thought it was more liable to become a
river. Or a waterfall.

I have to admit that by this stage I was becoming
worried about the last stretch of the climb to Shap
because I remembered it as being the steepest part.
How much steeper could it get?

I consoled myself that last time I had descended
solely on the A6. Perhaps Google was just being cruel
at this point, sending me up gradients double that
necessary. But I soon re-joined the A6 with no real
downhill to compensate for the 20% upward gradient
so assumed the A6 must have been similar.

I chugged up the hill, keeping a steady cadence
and sticking to a low gear, saving some reserves to
tackle the steepest bit at the top. The hill ground on
and on at 7-8% and I figured the top bit might be 12-
15%, based on the memory of dropping from the top

like a stone for the first mile or so. The gradient cranked up a notch to 9-10% for a long stretch and then started to ease off. Around the corner I was expecting to see the tarmac ramp up like a wall but it was flat! I had reached the top.

Hoorah!

I had a celebratory wee and texted home. I didn't hang around though because at 425m the temperature was low enough to cause my breath to fog. I dragged on my rain jacket for wind protection and hit the descent, which didn't last long enough to compensate for all the effort going up. The total ascent from the south is about 370m whereas the descent to Shap village is only 175m or so. Having said that, after a bit of up and down the A6 then drops a further 140m into Penrith, but spread over 13 miles it is hardly fast descending – but better than going up.

On the road to Penrith a sign to Lowther Castle caught my eye. I was born and grew up on Lowtherville Road in Ventnor on the Isle of Wight and had often wondered (but had never bothered to find out) where the name came from. Often road names are derived from the place they lead to, so the main road out of many towns is named after the next major town down the road. My mind was tired now and capable of

coming up with any number of crazy thoughts without the normal sanity blocks stopping them in their tracks so I twiddled away a mile or two contemplating the audacity of the plan to build a road from the Isle of Wight to Cumbria. There was most of England to cover, not to mention crossing the Solent. And in the end they had only ever completed ¼ mile before Lowtherville Road turned into Newport Road (the next major town on).

Yes, I was tired now and rambling like an idiot. Not out loud though. Not yet.

Shortly after I passed through Clifton, which claimed to be the site of the last battle to take place on English soil, in 1745. However, a number of places make this claim and it depends on how a battle is defined. Many historians consider the Clifton confrontation between the Jacobite rebels, led by Charles Edward Louis John Casimir Sylvester Severino Maria Stuart, aka Bonnie Prince Charlie, and the British Hanoverian government forces to be a mere skirmish. I'm not sure the 20 or so men from both sides that lost their lives would appreciate the nit picking though.

The A6 was getting busier as I approached Penrith and finding a place to wee was becoming an ever more urgent requirement. I tried sneaking down side roads but found them overlooked or equally busy with traffic. Just as things were getting desperate I arrived at a large roundabout. I didn't fancy cycling around it so used the cycle path which crossed the centre island. Slightly off the path was a wooded area obscured from the traffic (it was a *big* roundabout) which provided me with the privacy I needed.

In Memory of
Mrs Rose Clarke
Who lived & was loved in this
Village of Skelton for 85 Years
So rest your legs and enjoy your time here

Getting back on the bike I realised that I was not on the route anymore. I zoomed out and found that I had not been on the route for some time! For about the last 10 miles I had been blindly following the A6 whilst my route had turned off and was following a roughly parallel course on smaller lanes.

Despite my vow to follow the route I wasn't going to back track 10 miles and decided to pick it up again in Penrith, which I was now on the outskirts of.

I detoured to the local Morrisons to top up drinks, buy a few snacks and get a supply of batteries. Whilst the weather had been kind to me, with minimal rain, the light was gloomy most of the time and my rear end (light that is) had been flashing for the last 4 and a half days. The batteries usually last forever when I'm commuting but I was already on my spare set and the light was looking dim.

I was feeling hungry at this stage but didn't much fancy standing outside Morrisions stuffing my face so decided to find somewhere peaceful on the route with a nice comfy bench.

Before setting off in search of the route I did a quick check to see how I was progressing. It was now 13:49 and I was 57 miles in. That's 5 hours and 47 minutes total time which meant an average speed of a little under 10 mph. No matter what terrain I was covering I seemed to be averaging just under 10mph.

The sat nav led me via a cunning route out of Penrith following tiny lanes, up a steep hill, through a farm and onto some very peaceful, quiet lanes.

The lanes rolled gently along but my legs were tired and I was hungry. I just wanted to find a bench so I could stop and eat. I passed a bus stop but the shelter had no seat. Someone had a bench in their front garden but I'm not sure they would have been keen to come out and find a sweaty cyclist masticating on it. After what seemed an age I rolled into Skelton and spied a bench. It had a plaque on it which read, 'In memory of Mrs Rose Clarke who lived and was loved in this village of Skelton for 95 years so rest your legs and enjoy your time here.'

My legs needed a rest so I sat, ate, drank and thoroughly enjoyed my time there. I was amazed to realise that it was the first stop I had made on the whole trip that was specifically to eat and rest. Every other stop had been instigated by some other need like changing kit, stopping at shops, bypassing obstructions, taking notes, taking photos of nature, taking calls of nature etc... Thank you Rose.

Just outside the village I spotted some very tall radio masts. No great feat of observation, they were massive. I had no idea what they were but later discovered them to be part of the

BBC's Skelton Transmitting Station. In 1946 it was heralded as being the world's largest and most powerful (shortwave) radio station.

The main mast, at 365 metres high, is the tallest man made structure in the UK. The Shard is a mere 306 metres. No wonder I spotted it. I wouldn't fancy the job of putting the fairy on top at Christmas though.

After Skelton the road headed slightly downhill. With a tailwind I was able to maintain a good speed. At least I would have been able to if it wasn't for the frequent very steep sided dips down to watercourses. They were so regular and the land was so flat that I assumed they formed part of a drainage system. They had a draining effect on my legs anyway.

At the 73 mile mark I met an ominous blue sign for National Cycle Route 7 with 'off road' on it. I had looked as closely as I could at this section in Google before the start but had been unable to decide how 'off road' it was, Oscar not being able to go onto the paths. So the only way to find out was to cycle down it and see. I could always backtrack and follow the road if necessary.

The road quickly deteriorated to farm track. It had been raining almost continually for the last few weeks (at least it felt like it) and the track was thick with mud. Fortunately it was currently mostly dry but the tractors had gouged out deep tyre tracks with the mud between raised by several inches. It was very tough going on a road bike and in a couple of places I had to stop and walk to avoid falling.

Eventually I crawled out onto a hard surfaced road where I passed Lime House School. There was a lot of screaming emanating from over the walls. I assumed it was overly enthusiastic cheering for  some sporting activity but you do hear stories about private schools.

The 'road' only lasted a few metres and then I was back onto farm track. It was easier going here though. Until after a few hundred metres my route pointed me down a footpath. The sign warned of suckler cows that might be aggressive, especially if there were dogs present. I wondered how they might feel about bicycles.

After crossing a field where the farmer was producing black wrapped hay bales on a massive scale, I made it back to the road. I had probably saved myself a mile in distance by going 'off road' and lost

half an hour in time. I made a note to stick with the road in future and followed the B5299 into Carlisle.

I rode straight through Carlisle, only stopping long enough to take a picture of the gatehouse of Carlisle Castle. Although there has been a castle on the site since the days of William the Conqueror (or 'the Bastard' depending on your affiliation) the current keep dates from between 1122 and 1135. Being close to the border the castle has seen plenty of action and has changed hands many times during its history. Currently it is in the hands of English Heritage but I don't think they had to slaughter too many people to seize it.

I was out of Carlisle before I knew it and onto some small, mainly flat lanes. There was one busy section with large lorries but at that stage the road widened and was very straight so didn't prove to be a problem.

Spotting my first sign for Gretna my adrenaline started pumping and I found myself pushing hard on the pedals, keen to get to Scotland. It  was a wasted effort though. After making great time for a couple of miles I was halted at a level crossing, losing all the time gained. There's a lesson in there somewhere for the long distance cyclist.

Just three miles later I crossed the River Sark into Scotland and stopped at the border to take the obligatory photos of the sign and the marriage rooms: 10,000 marriages since 1840. I wondered how many had ended in divorce. Cynic.

I stopped in Gretna to top up my bottles thinking that it might be my last chance before Lockerbie and the end of the day. Stumbling around the shop on my cleats I was surprised that every person I heard talking had a Scottish accent. Sure, I was in Scotland but only just. There's no segregation and no wall or other physical barrier, so why isn't there some drift of cultures? Surely some people with English accents must live and work in Gretna just as some Scots must live and work in Carlisle, so why no blurring of the

lines? A mystery. Of course, there might be a good reason I only heard Scottish accents from those killing time in the shops, it was a work day.

I joined the B6357 outside of Gretna which dragged gradually uphill for 4 mile to join the B7076. This road snaked alongside the A74(M) for about 10 miles, crossing back and forth, until Lockerbie.

The last stretch from Gretna is all a bit of a blur. By that stage my brain was only working on essentials, like keeping safe, and not storing a lot of information. In a bid to get to the B&B before dark I had also stopped taking notes. But at the 100 mile point, somewhere on the B7076, I must have stopped for a wee and texted home. My text was timed at 17:59 and read:

> *Averaging just under 10 mph all day. Well, in yr face 'less than 10 mph'! 100 miles in 9 hrs 57 mins. Ha! Of course, just lost 5 minutes sending this :( Raining now. Hiding under road brg.*

Looking at the route after the event the road above the bridge must have been the A74(M), so plenty of space to hide from the rain.

The stop breathed some life into my legs, which was fortunate because I shortly hit the Ecclefechan hill. That's not swearing, although I was cursing at the time, it is a long long drag uphill through the town of Ecclefechan.

Looking for an excuse to stop I took some photos of the statute of Thomas Carlyle, who was born in Ecclefechan. I had no idea who he was but he was sat on a chair so assumed he was famous for introducing the chair to the Scottish. It turns out he was a teacher, historian and writer that had a great

influence on later writers such as Oscar Wilde.

Approaching Lockerbie I detoured from the route into the town itself where I found a chip shop and treated myself to a fish supper (when in Rome).

Sat on a wet bench in the late evening gloaming, with the only view being of the dispassionate traffic ebbing and flowing at the traffic lights, I was undecided how much of a treat it really was.

Even so, it was an effort to drag myself back on to the bike for the last couple of miles to the B&B, especially with the last couple of hundred metres being uphill.

Bike stowed, I was shown to my fantastically decorated room where I washed the day's woes down the shower plughole and set about my evening routines. The only downsides for the B&B were a lack of heating and a poor mobile signal. Not that the room was in any way cold, it just meant that I had to sit around in damp cycling clothes trying to get them dry. Although, as I sat watching the weather forecast for the next day, nibbling on the homemade biscuits thoughtfully provided, I wondered why I was bothering.

| Distance: | 111 miles | Av speed: | 12.8 mph |
|---|---|---|---|
| Time cycling: | 8:41 | Time overall: | 11:20 |
| Av heart rate: | 125 bpm | Calories burnt: | 3,610 |
| Total ascent: | 1,562 m | Max speed: | 35.5 mph |

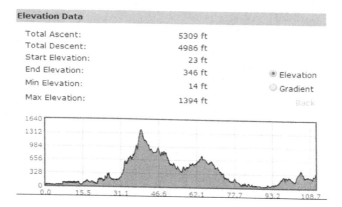

**Elevation Data**

| Total Ascent: | 5309 ft | |
|---|---|---|
| Total Descent: | 4986 ft | |
| Start Elevation: | 23 ft | |
| End Elevation: | 346 ft | ● Elevation |
| Min Elevation: | 14 ft | ○ Gradient |
| Max Elevation: | 1394 ft | Back |

# Chapter Eleven

## Day 6 – In search of the hills south of Edinburgh

The alarm went off and my mind rose out of a heavy sleep, slowly floating to the surface of a sea of cotton wool.

I switched the intrusive beeping off and tried to orientate myself. Where was I? Of yeah: cycle. LEJOG. What day? Lockerbie to Kinross. Zeal Monochorum, Frampton, Stafford, Condor Green, Lockerbie, Kinross... So Day 6. Only two more days to go, if I ignore today. Nearly there.

Part of me was awake enough to note I was still being optimistic, which was good. I could easily have decided I had only completed 5 days, which was still only just over half way.

What was I in for today? Hills. Lots of hills. The main reason I turned back on LEL was because I didn't want to get stuck high up in the hills south of Edinburgh, miles from anywhere. Most of today would be spent getting to Edinburgh so most of today must be hills.

What else? Rain. The weather forecast had promised 2-3 inches of rain. Lots of rain.

So, lots of hills and lots of rain.

I dragged my torso upright and swung my legs out of the bed. Trying to maintain my positive attitude I reminded myself that today was my shortest day; only 99 miles.

Bloody good thing, I thought as I creaked upright and lurched towards the toilet, like a zombie in a low budget 1980's movie, except none of my bits fell off.

I tried rubbing some life into my thighs but even so the descent of the stairs to the dining room was a stuttering affair with my knees refusing to bend and my thighs feeling like they were in clamps. They would definitely need a few miles to warm up. Hopefully the hills wouldn't start too soon.

I discovered that a Full Scottish Breakfast bore remarkable similarity to a Full English Breakfast. In fact the only difference I could determine was the name.

By this stage breakfast was very much an ordeal.

In Norman times criminal suspects were subjected to the Ordeal, which normally meant having to walk bare foot across nine red hot ploughshares, or picking a stone from the bottom of a barrel of boiling water or licking white hot iron. If the ~~victim~~ suspect suffered no injury then they had been protected by God and were innocent.

Eating breakfast wasn't quite that bad. In fact in normal conditions the breakfast would have been delicious but my whole body was pretty battered at this point. It was having enough trouble trying to cope with recovery without facing the prospect of dealing with the effort of digesting food as well. So I had to force it down, knowing that it would be vital in seeing me through the first couple of hours of cycling. At some point all that energy would drop into my legs and they would start to feel better.

I failed the ordeal, defeated by the toast, and my punishment was rain. Better than the hanging or mutilation the Norman suspect faced; if the Ordeal hadn't killed them already.

Setting off at 07:50 I was fully clad with arm and leg warmers, rain jacket and Rainlegs. I should point out, for the avoidance of doubt, that I was also wearing shorts and a cycling top. I was, after all, riding in Scotland, not Germany.

It was a mile or so from the B&B back to the route which continued along the B7076 the road that I had peeled off from the previous evening. It was a good road for cycling, having a wide strip beyond the solid white line at the edge of the carriageway that, on the whole, had an excellent surface. Despite looking like a major road it was also very quiet, most of the traffic being carried by the A74(M) running almost alongside.

There wasn't much to see though because the clouds had descended. I did spot a Moffat sign which had me intrigued. Apparently it was an 'Outstanding Conversation Town'. Did that mean it was so interesting that people talked about it a lot? Or did it have a conversation society where people went for a good chat? Perhaps they had won awards for the riveting conversation at their town council dinners? Of course the reality was I had misread the sign and it was really an 'Outstanding Conservation Town' (I doctored the picture). It was a good indication of where my head was though. [I photo shopped the picture.]

After 15 miles I hadn't found the hills. The road had bobbed up and down but I was still at roughly the same altitude as I had been at the start. The rain

came and went, like the hurried lover, and I stopped to peel off my rain jacket and my leg warmers and roll up my Rainlegs.

By chance I seemed to have stopped at the North/South divide, the road signs clearly defining the split. To the south the sky was brightening but to the north it was black with menace. I left the Rainlegs clipped around my waist.

The wide road and good surface should have seen my average speed crawl over 10 mph but tired legs and frequent stops to pull the rain jacket on and off curtailed that. After 2 hours I have covered 20 miles.

Stopping to take the rain jacket off once more I noticed a sign on a stile for a path leading off in to the hills. Upon it was, 'Come back safely, your family needs you.' It instantly put me back on my guard for the hills to come. Here was a clear warning that I was right to be concerned about getting stuck in these hills with a dodgy knee during LEL.

Gradually, gradually the tarmac headed upward and I kept anticipating a ramping up of the gradient. But it didn't seem to happen. I gained 200m in elevation but it took 10 miles, or 16km. That meant an average gradient of 1.25%. In other words, flat! The gradient of some of the canals had been steeper than that. Surely I hadn't given up on LEL to avoid this. The steepest gradient I had faced so far was 5%.

Before long I was heading gradually downhill and was getting annoyed at the lack of hills. It was a bizarre dichotomy because half of me desperately needed the hills to prove I was right to bail out of LEL but the other half was very thankful that Scotland was surprisingly flat.

To distract myself from the problem I started getting nit-picky and moaned internally about all the mud caked to my bike. It must have been getting steadily heavier the further north I had travelled. It occupied my mind for a few miles until I got fed up with the negativity and decided to do something about it. I stopped by the side of the road and found a handful of damp sphagnum moss, which I used to wipe the bike down. The mud was already wet from the rain so it came off fairly easily.

With a clean(er) bike I felt mentally much brighter, despite the fact that it was still lightly raining, on and off. I began to view the lack of hills in a better light. The LEL hadn't used this road to Edinburgh and probably had followed a much more arduous route. Of course there were lots of nasty hills in Scotland but my clever Google route had avoided them, much as it had further south: the country isn't really pan flat for hundreds of miles. Clever route. And clever sphagnum moss for cleaning my bike.

I should add bike cleaning to the list of uses for sphagnum moss, of which there are many. For instance it is a natural antiseptic and has been

used for centuries as a dressing for wounds. It was used extensively during the World Wars in field dressings to keep wounds clean. So I can feel secure in the knowledge that my bike shouldn't go septic.

The wind was picking up but fortunately it was still mainly from the South, so a tailwind. I had been extremely lucky with the wind on this trip. True, there had been a really strong headwind for the first two days but since then I have mainly benefitted from tailwinds.

The wind nearly let me down today though. It had just started raining again and as I pulled my rain jacket from my pocket the wind gusted and snatched it from my hand. At the time I was alongside and slightly above the A74(M) and images of it being whisked away across six lanes of traffic sprung instantly to mind. It had cost £150 (although I only paid half that but it was still bloody expensive) so I wasn't going to leave it like some pro cyclist casually chucking it in a hedge. Skittering across the tarmac on my cleats trying to avoid oncoming lorries was going to be difficult though.

It is amazing how much can zip through your mind

in a split second, even when you are feeling tired. Whilst I was thinking all that the jacket had managed to hook itself on my handlebar and I managed to grab it before the wind ripped it free again.

After days on the road fatigue and loneliness were beginning to have some psychological effect. I was starting to sing as I pedalled. Like an annoying toddler that only knows a few words of a song I kept repeating, "It never rains around here, it just comes pouring down," "Thunder only happens when it's raining," and "Why, why why, Delilah...."

It was also having a detrimental effect on my short term memory. I'd have a fleeting thought and stop to write it down only to find it had evaporated. Then I'd start pedalling again and it would reappear. Frustrated at having to keep stopping I'd decide to write it down next time I stopped but of course, by then it was long gone.

The monotony of the road was broken as I passed by Entrance F to the Clyde Wind Farm, followed a couple of miles later by Entrance E. Another couple of miles and Entrance D appeared, and so on. The wind farm must have been huge but I hadn't seen a single turbine. They had done an excellent job of hiding it.

Of course there might have been a forest of them on the tops of the hills, veiled by the rain laden, low lying clouds. During the Scottish element of our soggy holiday in Cumbria and Scotland, my wife and I hadn't seen a hill top all week. The cloud had remained at 150m, or lower for our entire visit.

I wasn't doing much better this time and was conscious that I hadn't managed to take any photos of the landscape so far. I wheeled uphill past a farm (normal

not wind) and held an internal debate about whether to stop and take a photo or not. By the time I decided that I should try to get some pictures I was well beyond the best shot and had to freewheel back down the hill to take it. Plodding back up the hill I wondered whether it had been worth the effort: it just showed gloomy.

Cruising down the other side of the hill the wind swirled the skirts of the cloud and the base of a massive windmill flashed into sight and was gone again. I stopped and got the camera out, waiting for another flash of the skirts: clearly the wind farm was up there somewhere.

I waited for several minutes, at best capturing the murky outline of a single windmill. In the end, mindful of time, I gave up and pedalled on. Just as I got up to cruising speed (about three minutes) the clouds lifted and I had to throw out the anchor and scrabble for the camera.

The trouble was, the camera just couldn't cope with the low light conditions. I had toyed with the idea of taking my primary camera but decided that being jolted around on canal paths and worse for eight days probably wouldn't be very good for it. It was also too bulky and heavy.

Yet, at least I had glimpsed the wind farm, which I could now imagine marching across the hills, deep into Scotland.

Nearly 30 miles from the day's start my route and the A74(M) diverged. The A74(M) headed north west towards Glasgow whilst I continued along the B7076 until it joined the A702 a few miles later, heading north east towards Edinburgh and those hills.

But the hills still hadn't arrived. There were small ups and downs but the road remained fairly level. Despite my positive spin on things I was still caught between disappointment and relief. I needed the hills as justification for bailing LEL but didn't really want to climb any: perhaps if I could just see some roads heading up into the hills that I didn't actually have to follow?

On the positive side the weather was definitely brightening and there had even been a yellow tinge to the cloud now and then. All my rain gear was off and stowed and I was down to shorts and short sleeves. In fact, bearing in mind I was in Scotland and it was October, it was getting warm. Then the sun stabbed down through the distant drizzle, sparking a brief lived rainbow. I stopped to take a picture and noted that I

was 40 miles into the day after 3 hours and 40 minutes, so nearly 11mph: woo hoo! A definite bright moment.

A few miles down the road I followed behind a road sweeper (a motorised one, I wasn't going *that* slowly). He would extend his brushes and swish the road edge clean until I caught up to him whereupon he would retract the brushes, zoom up the road a bit and sweep some more, until I caught up again. We danced thus together for a few miles until I thought he was probably getting fed up with me so I stopped.

I took the opportunity for a slightly longer break and did all the little tasks I'd been hanging onto for the last few miles: I had a wee, made some notes, ate a cereal bar and called home. I also transferred my drink from my back bottle to my nearly empty front bottle, it being easier to grab the front one. This was not as simple as swapping the bottles over. The frame on my bike was so compact that the rear bottle cage didn't have enough clearance to hold anything bigger than a 500ml bottle. So I had to pour the drink from the smaller bottle to the larger one held in the front cage, something I couldn't do on the move.

The whole process took about 15 minutes, which meant the sweeper would be miles down the road, never to be seen again.

I clambered back onto the bike and set off around the corner. And there, not 300 metres down the road was the sweeper, parked in a layby, the driver having a tea break.

Pressing on, the weather brightened further to the point of sustained sunshine, almost bright enough to cast shadows.

With brighter weather my eyes lifted from the road and I spotted some hay bales, which are always worth photographing. I noticed that these hay bales had none of the discipline of the black plastic clad BDSM ones back in Cheshire that had all been lined up in a row.

All the stopping and starting was taking a toll on my average speed, which after 50 miles had dropped back to my customary 10mph. More problematic

though was the distinct lack of shops. Five hours into the ride I was running empty and getting worried. I hadn't passed through a town all day and as far as I knew there might not be one until Edinburgh, still about 30 miles away.

Spotting a small white cottage by the side of the road I stopped to see if there was anyone home. There was no reply so I nosed around the back to see if there was an outside tap. No. I could see a tap in the kitchen through the window. Desperate I tried the door. Locked.

Cursing I got back on the bike and rolled down the road to the small settlement of Libberton. I stopped by a row of houses and knocked on the door of the first one. No reply. I tried the second. Same result. Third: still no one in. Mmmm, burglars could clean up here.

Trying a different approach I scanned the roof tops. Lo! Just around the corner smoke was rising. I knocked on the door. The lady that answered looked at me with some suspicion over the baby she was clutching protectively to her chest. I couldn't blame her, I probably didn't look too good after five and a half days on the road and I don't expect they see too many haggard, lycra clad blokes in Libberton.

I explained my plight and whilst she continued to frown she swung the babe to her hip and took my empty, slightly sticky bottles. The door swung closed with a thud and I waited, rocking back on my heels to stretch my calves.

My calves had a good long stretch before the door opened again. My saviour had returned with my bottles. They were full of precious water and sparkling clean.

Devoid of babe my benefactor seemed less guarded and broke into a half smile at my perfuse thanks. She asked me what I was doing. When dealing with someone that hasn't spoken since breakfast, if you ignore loud singing to self, and very little in the last few days, this is a mistake.

After a couple of minutes of my prattle her eyes glazed over and I could tell it was time to leave. Thanking her again I retreated to my bike. I scooted around the corner before getting out my bag of powder and converting the water to energy drink in case she thought I was doing something dodgy.

In theory I was halfway through the day so, freshly stocked with drink I probably had enough to get me to the end. Nevertheless I decided to top up at any opportunity to make sure I didn't get dehydrated.

Ironically 2 miles down the road I entered the small town of Carnwath. For such a small town it was remarkably well endowed with shops. There was a bank, a hardware store, a newsagents, a beauty shop, a pharmacy, a wine merchant, a post office, a premier convenience store right next door to a co-op, a Chinese takeaway, 2 pubs and a car wash. It seemed that all the shops for miles around had decided to up sticks and relocate here. True to my word I drained one of my bottles and refilled.

Still searching for those elusive hills I sloshed out of Carnwath and began to climb. I climbed for nearly 7 miles but only gained 110 metres in altitude, topping out at 323 metres. I use the term 'climb' but in reality it was a gradient of 1.1%, which is pretty much flat.

The climb was along the A70 which was very quiet. I stopped at a sign for Lang Whang. If it wasn't for the Central Scotland Countryside Trust bit

on the sign I might have thought I had gone awry and ended up in China. My wife Googled it and discovered that Lang Whang is old Scots for "Long way" or "Long Bootlace" and generally refers to the A70. Well, that made sense, I was on the A70, but I couldn't help thinking that Lang Whang might also be boastful old Scots for what they keep under their kilts.

My wife also discovered from Wikipedia that, "Much of the road is over elevated, desolate moorland; it ascends several times on its course to heights over 1000 feet above sea level. Because the wind enjoys an easy and uninterrupted passage over its length, in winter the road is frequently closed by snow, even by modest snowfalls. The road passes elevated farmland and grouse moor and presents extensive views over central Scotland to the north." I could attest to windy: there were a lot of windmills about. Luckily no snow. In fact it was an unbelievable 21.8 C!

The wind was being a Mercurial beast today: at some points it would be blasting me along from the rear, then it would switch in an instant to a headwind and then disappear altogether. I could only think it was due to the topology of the landscape, the wind funnelling through glens and getting turned around and about. There is often the same effect on Dartmoor. At the moment I was driving into a headwind so, looking for an excuse to stop, I took a picture of some cows and windmills. It seemed that most of my photos featured windmills or hay bales.

When I pulled out my camera, the plastic bag I stored it in to keep the rain off rustled and the cows' heads came up. They plodded over to me looking expectant. I could only assume the farmer fed them tasty supplements from plastic bags that rustled. They looked at me with big brown, sad eyes and I felt a bit mean, not having anything to give them. I chatted with them for a while but they seemed unimpressed with my cycling efforts and eventually wandered off.

The road started heading downhill and with only 15 miles or so to Edinburgh I began to wonder whether I had conquered the alleged hills before Edinburgh. I was at just over 300 metres elevation and the crossing of the River Forth north of Edinburgh must be at close to sea level. If the descent was a similar gradient to the ascent, about 1%, then the 'downhill' would last all the way there.

Turning off the Lang Whang I was tearing down a gloriously long, straight downhill along the B7006 when my sat nav warned me I was off route. Glancing down I noted that I should have turned right so hauled on the brakes and did a U turn. Grinding

back up the hill I reminded myself to change down gears before making the turn if it happened again.

When I regained the turn I was disappointed to note that the road was in fact a track. It was the first off road I had faced for some time and my butt wasn't relishing the prospect.

For those of a squeamish disposition please skip to the next paragraph. Whilst I hadn't suffered majorly from saddle sore on this trip I had spent some contorted moments each evening lancing pustules in rather sensitive areas. If anyone has ever wondered what practical purpose the 'removing stones from hooves' tool has on a Swiss Army Knife I can highly recommend it as a lancing tool. The tip of mine seems to be far sharper than a needle and has the required weight to drive through taut skin. I can also recommend Metanium nappy rash cream, applied nightly to clear up any problems whilst you sleep. It contains titanium and, for a cyclist, any titanium add on is a boon. In the day I was applying a thick layer of Sudocrem, another antiseptic nappy rash cream which also acts as a lubricant to ease friction between shorts and sensitive areas.

Okay, you can look again now.

The track wasn't too bad but dragged on for some time. I was also annoyed that I had missed out on that lovely descent and made a note to try and avoid this track if possible: if it annoyed me it would annoy anyone else who might follow the route.

However, a few miles down the road I decided I would trade 30 miles on the track for the 3 miles I had to negotiate on the manic A899 through Livingstone. The road was a crazy busy, dual carriageway with no space beyond the solid white line. It had a continuous succession of major arteries joining and leaving it, some two lanes wide themselves, with cars and lorries diving on and off. But the worst parts were the two major roundabouts that I had to cross, the last being a 270 degree turn onto the A89. There was no cycle path at any point and clearly was not a route for cycling along.

The A89 should have been worse but fortunately it had a very good cycle path along the entire length I had to cycle. However, by then my nerves were kind of shot. Praying that the roads wouldn't be like that all the way to the Forth Bridge I stopped at a services to calm down and re-fuel.

As it happens the route to the bridge was quiet. I left the A89 over a footbridge onto a quiet path that led to residential streets. They in turn led to a cycle path to and over the bridge. The only concern was that my sat nav was informing me that it had lost its link to satellites, which left me blind in terms of my route. I had to dig around in my bag and find the paper route that I had stowed away on day 2. It then took some time to work out where I was on the route, not helped by the fact that I had ridden off route under satellite black out. The situation was compounded because my head had decided it had done enough by that stage: it was 15:50, I was 80 miles and 8 hours in (still 10 mph!) and my concentration powers were waning.

I vaguely knew which way north was so decided to just keep heading that way. I would either hit a street shown on the paper route or the River Forth. From there I would be able to navigate by sight.

As it happens I found the route within a few

hundred metres and the sat nav remade contact with satellites shortly after. A few twists and turns brought me to a vista of the Forth Road Bridge. I had a good look but couldn't see the other three [BaDoom Tish].

Bridges seem short and flat when you drive across them. Cycling across you can appreciate what huge feats of engineering they are. The Forth Road Bridge was a mile and a half long and humped at a reasonable gradient. It made for a steady climb followed by a rapid descent.

I stopped halfway down the descent to take some photos of the Forth Rail Bridge, curious as to what the buildings on the island near one of the sets of piers was. Normally I hold the camera against any available solid surface to help stabilise the image and avoid hand shake blur. In this instance it was pointless. Every time a car went past the bridge shuddered. Whenever a lorry went by, the handrail I was trying to use as a stabiliser would visibly move by almost a centimetre.

In the end I gave up trying to take a clear picture because the rain had started again. I hauled on my jacket and set off on the last 18 miles of the day.

Incidentally, the island is called Inchgarvie and there have been buildings upon it for hundreds of years, dating back to the Middle Ages. The current buildings are a conglomerate of those through time and have been used in times past for various functions including: as a fort, a syphilis refuge, a prison, a chapel and a quarantine hospital. Latterly the island

itself has been extended to form a foundation for one of the Forth Rail Bridge's cantilevers.

Forging on through the rain I eventually found all the hills south of Edinburgh: they were north of Edinburgh. I crawled up and up and up with some biting gradients. The rain was steady and I was tired and my mood was getting darker as the light began to fade.

The climbing eventually took its toll and my knee began to give. There were stabbing pains behind my kneecap that I couldn't ignore. With reluctance I climbed off and dug through my bag to find my knee support, last worn a couple of weeks before. Should I have felt some sense of gratification pulling it on? Surely it proved that hills would have been too much for my damaged knee and

I was exonerated for doing the sensible thing on LEL. Not really: it was the other bloody knee!

I ground on and eventually came to a forest and climbed still higher. The gradient steepened as I weakened until suddenly the climb was over and I was plunging down a very steep descent. It could have been a very rapid descent but I had the only car for miles around just in front of me and they were being rather timid. It was too twisty and I was too tired to try any overtaking manoeuvres so I wore my brake pads down behind them.

It was starting to get dark as I neared the finish but my eyes perked up at an intriguing road sign pointing the direction to Crook of Devon. How bizarre to come most of the way across the country to find somewhere called Crook of Devon. It had a story behind it that name; something from bygone days. Had a notorious highway robber from Devon gone into hiding there? Did a Devonshire man once live there who was thought of as a swindler by the locals? Maybe the name derived from a shepherd's crook and a local farmer had once had an unusual flock of Devon sheep. Or perhaps a Bishop's crook? Did a Devon bishop once have a palace there?

**《 Crook of Devon  4 》**

It kept my mind away from feeling exhausted as I pedalled the last couple of miles into Kinross where I purchased a Meal Deal at the Co-op to eat at the B&B.

It turns out that the source of the name is much more mundane: it derives from the sudden angle (crook) which the River Devon makes near the village. More intriguing than anything I had managed to conjure however, is the fact that it was famous in the

17th century for its witch burnings. Apparently the witches were strangled and burnt at the stake in a field near the village hall. These days we have to settle for a fete or a Bring and Buy sale.

I arrived at the B&B at 18:02. That was just over 10 hours for 102 miles on the road. 10 mph. What a surprise! The strange thing seemed to be, no matter how I was feeling throughout the day (or the last few days) I seemed to be moving at an almost constant speed. That was encouraging because it implied I wouldn't slow down. But it did mean that the last day of 140 miles would take 14 hours.

But that was a worry for another day. Saturday to be precise. I had to get through Friday first.

In the meantime I had the sanctuary of my B&B to try and recover in. Having gone through my evening rituals of showering, washing my clothes and sorting my kit, I slumped on the thoughtfully provided sofa. Munching through an egg and bacon sandwich (a strange choice given all those breakfasts), crisps and drink I watched the local weather forecast. Apparently there had been several inches of rain in some areas. I frowned at this. True, there had been a couple of hours at the beginning of the day and another couple at the end but none of it had been particularly heavy. If they glorified that by calling it several inches I have to say I barely felt it or recall the experience: as the actress said to the bishop.

The Meal Deal went down well and I realised that I hadn't eaten anything since it had started raining on the Forth Road Bridge. Little wonder the last two hours of cycling had been tough if I hadn't been stoking the engine.

Even so, the Pot Noodle was hard to force down. Maybe I should have bought more than one flavour. I was heartily sick of Bombay Bad Boy, partly because it conjured up images of dogs. Dogs and noodles are not a good combination, unless you're...no better not go there.

The large bar of chocolate went down easily enough though.

After phoning home for a moan and noting down my stats for the day I was faced with one last dilemma: which bed should I sleep in, the one on the left or the right?

| Distance: | 102 miles | Av speed: | 13 mph |
|---|---|---|---|
| Time cycling: | 7:49 | Time overall: | 10:12 |
| Av heart rate: | 123 bpm | Calories burnt: | 3,167 |
| Total ascent: | 1,373 m | Max speed: | 35.2 mph |

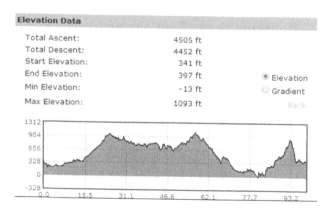

Elevation Data

| Total Ascent: | 4505 ft | |
|---|---|---|
| Total Descent: | 4452 ft | |
| Start Elevation: | 341 ft | |
| End Elevation: | 397 ft | ● Elevation |
| Min Elevation: | -13 ft | ○ Gradient |
| Max Elevation: | 1093 ft | Back |

# Chapter Twelve

## Day 7 – Highland Highlights

I woke bright and early. Well, early anyway. I didn't feel bright and it was certainly not bright outside. It was, in fact, particularly gloomy.

Putting the kettle on to prepare for an early caffeine boost I tried to dredge from my memory what today's ride entailed. Failing, I grabbed my paper route and retreated under the covers to wait out the 10 minutes it was likely to take the tiny kettle to boil the cup full of water.

Of course, I was heading into the Highlands. Well, if yesterday was spent in search of hills I *knew* there would be hills today; there was a clue in the name. Towards the end of the day I would be passing through the ski resort of Aviemore, which must be high up, certainly a lot higher than the 120 metres altitude I was starting at.

Never mind. Today was my penultimate day. I just needed to get through today and then it was one final push to the end. Admittedly that final push was 140 miles but I had ridden most of the roads the other way on my JOGLE and knew there were no real nasties, other than the two hills near Helmsdale I have mentioned before.

As the kettle rumbled towards boiling point I noted that today's distance was 110 miles. A bit more than yesterday so I had better chomp through breakfast and then try and get some miles in early; maybe even push against the pedals a little.

The stairs were solidly built and made no groan or

squeak but I managed to creak all the way down them. My knee was feeling stiff but not as bad as it had been at the end of the previous day. I raged a bit at the irony of the other knee going. Perhaps I had been subconsciously favouring it?

The dining room was a bastion of calm and the view out onto the garden was splendid. The garden was only small but was meticulously maintained and had a display of herbaceous flowers and plants that made it feel like July not October.

Either the garden had settled me into the right frame of mind or my body was getting used to the rigours and routines of the tour because I managed to demolish the breakfast with something approaching an appetite. I crammed in as many calories as possible, remembering the difficulties I had finding shops the day before (and on most days come to that).

Pedalling away just before 8am, the road was wet but there was nothing falling out of the sky. Apart from the clouds. They had plummeted to ground level so I had to engage front and rear lights.

The road went up and down a bit over the first few miles before plunging down to nearly sea level. It was an exhilarating descent (I reached my highest speed of the trip at 46 mph) but anyone who has ever cycled very far will be familiar with the dichotomous emotions of racing down hills. There is the joy of swooping down, effortlessly eating up the road as the air rushes through your hair (or buffets against your helmet). However, this is nearly always accompanied by a grinning demon sat on your

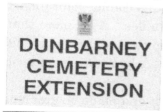

DUNBARNEY CEMETERY EXTENSION

shoulder whispering that you're going to have to grind your way back up again soon. Perversely the cycling rule of physics is, 'What comes down, must go up.'

I tried to banish the negative thoughts but it was difficult with nothing much to look at. Visibility was down to a few metres in places so there was very little in the way of distraction, just road signs. So I decided to play a game of that classic, 'Who Can Spot the Scottish Place Name with the Highest Scrabble Score.'

Kinross, my starting town, scored 11 but the early front runner was Dunzie with a score of 16. This was shortly equalled by Duncrievie before being usurped by Wicks O'Baiglie with a forceful showing of 25.

One of the more unusual signs was to Horsemill. Whilst only worth 14 I couldn't get the image of a large mill grinding down horses out of my head – messy!

The sign that really put a smile on my face though was the one to 'Pert', which I assumed was meant to read Perth (10).

Approximately 10 miles into the day, just before Bridge of Earn (19) I cycled up to the very French looking Dunbarney Cemetery. It was a walled affair a few hundred metres outside of the town with an ambiguous temporary road sign just outside the entrance: Dead Slow. Was it trying to say that I should cycle dead slowly, that I was in the presence of the dead so should slow down or that the dead were slow?

There was little time to contemplate the conundrum because my mind was already working on the Dunbarney Cemetery Extension next door. I wondered whether they had needed planning permission to build an extension. Surely most of the accommodation was underground and the extra residents would hardly be a drain on the council's resources. Also, if you went to purchase a plot did someone say, "...and of course you will be staying in our newly appointed extension, fully modernised and away from the noise and bustle of the main cemetery."? And, where was Dunbarney anyway? The town I was entering was Bridge of Earn.

The confusion continued as I passed Dunbarney Primary School (which had a very appropriate bench outside) and a sign to Dunbarney Parish Church. I checked the sign on the way out of town: Bridge of Earn.

It turns out that Dunbarney is the name of the parish that contains Bridge of Earn.

In Perth the route kept me to cycle paths shared with dog walkers. If the dogs had walked that would have been fine but the Perth variety seemed to be mental, chasing just in front of my wheel and leaping about in far too excited a manner for my liking. In a word they were far too pert.

To let one particularly pert dog move away I stopped to read a sign about the Bridges of Perth. Whilst there were records of a bridge as far back as the

12th century there had been a 150 year gap when there had been no bridge after it had been swept away by floodwater in 1621. The bridge was rebuilt in 1771 under the direction of Smeaton. This was a name that caught

my eye because he is famous for building the Eddystone Lighthouse that now sits on Plymouth Hoe, half a mile from the office where I work.

Cycling under the last arch of the bridge and along the cycle path I thought about the fate of the builder of the first light house on the Eddystone Rocks, Henry Winstanley. Despite my earlier rant about engineers being cited as constructing things rather than designing them I feel safe in calling him a builder because he was at least on the lighthouse supervising repairs when it was totally obliterated in the Great Storm of 1703. No traces of him or the five other men on the lighthouse were ever found. Brave men indeed to be building a wooden lighthouse on a rock barely out of the sea 22 miles from shore.

A few miles beyond Perth the temperature was rising. It was 10:00 and time to take my leg warmers off. I was at the 22 miles point so was averaging my customary 10 mph.

The road was climbing now. It wasn't very steep but my knee was niggling and I didn't want to push too hard and put it under strain. I was hoping that if

I could twiddle away in a low gear the pain would go away. To help matters I stopped to take some vitamin I.

Not much further down the road I was stopping again, this time at a shop in Bankfoot (17). I topped up my bottles with Iron Bru (when in Scotland...). Marvellous stuff: it looks and tastes like rusty girders – distinctive. I also had to put my knee support on.

Just 10 minutes later I had stopped again. My knee was getting decidedly painful now. I swallowed a couple of extra pain relief tablets and wondered whether I was facing defeat. I had stopped in the most clichéd sounding place possible for such thoughts: Waterloo! Sing along now – ♪ Waterloo. ♫ Finally facing my Waterloo. ♪ Wo wo ♫ wo wo ♫ Waterloo...

Believe it or not there are seven Waterloos in the UK, four in England, one in Wales and two in Scotland. There are forty five other Waterloos around the world, thirty one of them in USA. There was me thinking Waterloo was in Belgium. But then, I thought Perth was in Australia. I could have been on a tour across the world rather than the country. No wonder my knee was starting to give way.

I took it very easy for the next few miles, stopping at Rohallion Loch (19) to admire the autumn colours that were just coming in. In a couple more weeks the view would be glorious.

Much to the relief of my knee the road started to head downhill for the next four miles into Dunkeld. Although a small place, with a population of a little over a thou-

sand, some argue that Dunkeld is technically a city because it has a Cathedral. In fact in the 9<sup>th</sup> century it was proclaimed the first ecclesiastical capital of Scotland, by Scotland's 1<sup>st</sup> king, Kenneth MacAlpin.

Detouring slightly off the route to view the cathedral I spotted a sign which declared, 'Blind People Drive Slowly'. I wasn't quite sure if it was a warning or merely a comment. If a warning it seemed fairly pointless – blind drivers wouldn't be able to see it.

It was very similar to a sign I had passed earlier in the day warning, 'Children Please Drive Carefully'. I would have liked to have thought that they weren't driving at all but thereafter had kept my eyes peeled so as to avoid any infant driven automobiles.

Climbing out of Dunkeld my route directed me off the road and through the most splendid gateway for a cycle route I have even seen. It was the drive of the Hilton Dunkeld House, once the

summer residence of the Dukes of Atholl. To avoid lowering the tone with a load of scruffy cyclists, in the final approach to the hotel the route branched onto an off road track and out of sight.

Having dealt mostly with road for a couple of days the off road was a bit of a strain in the butt region and I spent some time out of the saddle. At least it took my mind off my knee.

In keeping with the theme for the route, after the calm, if battering, track I emerged directly onto the busy A9. Much like my mental image of an archetypal Scotsman, it was rough, hairy and extremely dangerous if you take your eyes off it for a moment.

I could have followed the A9 for the next 180 miles all the way to the A99, then it would just be another 33 mile to John O'Groats. Thankfully I was only on it for about 9 miles before turning off into Pitlochry (19). The last 3 miles were dual carriageway and were not too bad but I welcomed the release of tension I felt on the minor road.

Pitlochry had an abundance of shops but they were all aimed at tourists. Without stopping to take a full inventory there were at least three knitwear shops, two golfing shops, 2 outdoor gear shops, two clear-ance/remnant outlets, various gift shops, numerous cafés and restaurants a gallery and a Christmas Emporium, which I would have thought would be quite seasonal [it was, in fact, closed]. The only shops to service the needs of locals that I spotted were a wine shop, a whisky shop and a 'drinkmonger' (why not, you get fishmongers right?). And for the aftereffects, be it hangover or pregnancy tests, two chemists.

The road through Pitlochry and a few miles beyond climbed continually, albeit gradually until a short, steep descent wiped out half my altitude gain, dropping me into Killiecrankie (23). It was my second highest scoring place name so far but I couldn't get the thought of someone throttling Wee Jimmy Krankie out of my head (anyone under the age of 30 will probably have to Google that). Interestingly (or not) Janette Tough, who played Wee Jimmy Krankie, was born in Queenzieburn about 70 miles south. A score of 32!

The road bumped up and down for a few miles and I passed a sign warning me of Red Squirrels! Damn, I knew I should have brought a Taser with me. I'd better watch out.

Despite the mist there hadn't been any rain but in Bridge of Tilt (19) that all changed. Cycling along, minding my own business, a light rain of gravel fell upon me. The lady trying to scare birds off her garden was most apologetic though.

Shortly after I suffered my first (and only) puncture. Ironically, after all the off road tracks, it was on the road. I lost 20 minutes changing the inner tube and cleaning my hands off on some sphagnum moss.

The road had been

climbing slowly since Bridge of Tilt but suddenly ramped up. I passed one or two houses, rounded a corner and saw the road rising up in front of me. 'Urgh Ah!' thought I. 'Here comes the climb into the Highlands.'

A couple of hundred metres up the slope I came to an ominous sign. Apparently the cycle track climbed to 457m and I could be caught out by sudden changes in the weather. There was no food or shelter for 30 km. I checked my bottles – nearly empty. They might have warned me a few miles back where the last shop was!

Looking back down the hill for inspiration I remembered the few houses I had passed. Turning the bike around I rolled back down the hill to the first one. Nobody in. I continued to the next. Nobody in. Next. Ditto. Last one. Nobody there.

Bugger!

At my normal 10mph that meant two hours before I could fill my bottles. Today I was travelling even more slowly: 6½ hours from the start I had only achieved 55 miles, about 8½mph.

WARNING
Drumochter Summit
Cycle track climbs to 457m
Weather conditions deteriorate without warning and can be severe even in summer
No food or shelter for 30km
No snow clearance or gritting on cycle track

Retracing my tyre tracks I passed the sign and trundled onto the track. Fortunately the gradient slackened back down to very little.

Conscious of not having much drink I became thirsty. I debated whether it was better to ration my drink or just finish it off and decided it was better inside me than inside the bottle.

Rather than descend into a gloom worrying about dehydration, I tried to look on the positive side. I was cycling through some amazing countryside, it hadn't rained all day (except gravel) and the major plus was that the pain killers had kicked in and my knee felt ok.

Buoyed by positive thinking I floated up the slopes and soon came to a house, set back from the road with a gravel drive. After lots of practise at off road cycling I risked skidding through the gravel and headed towards the open door: a good sign. A large, snarling dog thundered through it trailing spittle: a bad sign. I leapt off the bike and used it as a feeble shield between me and Snarling Hackle Breath. It probably wasn't his name but it suited him.

I was pondering retreating to the road, fending the dog off like a lion tamer, when a lady appeared at the door and called the beast to heel. He lopped off and sat calmly at her feet. I approached cautiously, keeping the bike well positioned, and explained my plight.

The lady nodded and said she had cyclists coming in all the time, being one of the only houses for miles around. She asked me to relinquish my shield and come into the kitchen where I could fill my bottles from the tap.

Edging past Snarling Hackle Breath I was tempted to reach out and pat his head. A slight curling of the lip made me refrain. There was a glow deep in his eyes that said, "If my mistress wasn't here you'd be dinner!"

Bottles filled, rather than risk a humiliating spill on the gravel I walked back up the drive, grinding my cleats away. Re-united with the road I waved as the lady stepped back into the house. In an instant Snarling

Hackle Breath was bounding through the gravel towards me. Fearing the worst I sprinted off as fast as I could but once I was clear of the property the dog stopped, shouting at me never to come back again. Well, I wouldn't.

Not much further on I spotted my first red squirrel. After my dog encounter it didn't look very threatening but I kept a safe distance away. I remember well the warning of Tim the Enchanter in Monty Python and the Holy Grail: *"But follow only if you are men of valour. For the entrance to this cave is guarded by a monster, a creature so foul and cruel that no man yet has fought with it and lived. Bones of full fifty men lie strewn about its lair ... therefore sweet knights if you may doubt your strength or courage come no further, for death awaits you all with nasty pointy teeth."* True, he was talking about a rabbit but they are very similar to

squirrels in the nasty pointy teeth department.

The track was excellent. It had a really good surface and ghosted alongside the A9, sometime quite close and at others a hundred metres or so away. It bucked up and down like a rollercoaster (albeit a rollercoaster for toddlers) and there was the odd wooden bridge crossing of a stream to negotiate but on the whole it was a good path.

It was certainly better

than the A9, which looked rather lethal, inspiring me to stop and take a photo of the 'Danger of Death – Keep Off' sign nailed to an electricity pylon juxtaposed against a lorry as it thundered by. But after a while the constant up and down of the track began to take its toll. Every time I had to go down I would look wistfully at the constant 1-2% slope of the A9. There was no doubt I was doing a lot more climbing and up steeper gradients than I would be on the road. But on the other hand there was less danger of death.

I relieved the boredom of the climb by stopping to talk to a horny Scot but he didn't seem much inter-ested in my plight, blithely chewing the cud throughout my monologue.

By the time I reached Drumochter

Summit I had re-named the climb as the Bitchin Pass. Fourteen miles of up and down, but gradually overall up, had triggered the pain in my knee again and I stopped to reload on painkillers.

Bizarrely I had made good time on the climb. It was just after 15:30 so my average had actually risen to over 9 mph, which was probably why my knee was getting sore again.

The sign at the top claimed an altitude of 462m but my sat nav only registered it as 459m. Perhaps they were bigging it up. I had been expecting higher elevations than this in the Cairngorms, it was after all a skiing area, as evidenced by a particularly innovative bench on the climb up made out of old skis. Admittedly I was only on the edge of the Cairngorms but even Dartmoor has roads higher up than 459m.

Despite the warning signs the weather was not severe, it was in fact 17 Celsius and sunny. There were no ferocious red squirrels either, unless they were hiding in ambush behind the sign, ready to leap out and tear my throat out with their 'nasty pointy teeth'.

My total ascent so far today was 1001m whilst my total descent was only 659m. That meant I had 342m of stored energy on board, ready to be unleashed on the downhill. When I'm climbing I find it helps if I think in these terms. Every metre I manage to claw upward means I have a free metre on the way back down again.

The track on the descent was similar to the ascent, bucking up and down with twists and turns, bridges and cattle grid. But on the whole it was downward and an hour and ten minutes later I was 17 miles further along the road in Newtonmore, topping up on drink. I was feeling tired and had bought a Monster energy (caffeine) drink to perk me up and help me through the last 24 miles. My average speed had zoomed up to 10½ mph so if I could maintain that I was only about 2½ hours from the B&B. That would likely still be after dark though, somewhere around 19:00. The only problem was that I noticed the sat naff was still showing that I had 35 miles to go, which would mean 20:00 or later.

The cycle through the Cairngorms was probably the highlight of the tour, in particular a stretch through Inshriach Forest (26) where the autumn colours were just beginning to splash the scene with reds and golds. The scenery was constantly breath taking and the road just rolled gently up and down. I tried several times to capture the atmosphere on film (well, flash card) but my camera was not up to the task.

The best shot I managed was of Ruthven Barracks, the smallest but best preserved of four barracks built in 1719 to guard the Cairngorms after the 1715 Jacobite rising. Set on an old castle mound from earlier fortifications, dating back as far as the early 1200s, the Barracks dominate the landscape.

 They were ruined by the Jacobites on their retreat after the Battle of Culloden in 1746. After the skirmish of

Clifton it seemed I was following in Bonnie Prince Charlie's steps.

I don't know whether Bonnie Prince Charlie ever went to Aviemore, I've never heard of him being a keen skier, but I had to pass through it to get to my B&B. Unfortunately there was a storm sat over the town. The words of the story I read to my youngest the night before setting out (We're Going on a Bear Hunt) came to mind: We can't go over it, we can't go under it, we'll have to go through it.

The light was already fading and in the torrential rain it was virtually dark when I arrived in Aviemore shortly after 6pm. I had cycled 105 miles which meant I should have only had 5 more to go. But sat naff was still showing 17! There was a map in Aviemore showing the terrain and it looked like my last few miles would be predominantly uphill. There was something ominously called Slochd Summit to go over. That didn't sound good.

I phoned home and asked my wife, AKA Remote Support Unit, if she could call the B&B and say I might not be in until after 20:00. They were aware that I was cycling and I had said I might be in after dark so foresaw no problems. No doubt the sat naff was wrong anyway.

The road began a gradual climb but five miles later there was no sign of a B&B. I decided the sat nav must be right and I had read the mileage for the wrong day or had simply written it down incorrectly on my route sheet.

My energy levels were in a trough and I was starting to shake. I've been told this is the body's reaction as it

transitions from using energy from the gut (food) and easily accessible stored energy in the muscles and liver (glycogen) to the more difficult to use energy stored as fat. Although I could do with losing a few pounds this was not the time for it so I stopped and crammed down some food and drink. I still had over an hour to cycle and needed to make sure my body was fuelled.

Calling home my wife told me that the landlady had not been happy when she heard I wouldn't get there until 8pm. Ironically this was the only B&B where I had pre-booked an evening meal. Apparently it was now congealing in the oven. They normally lock the door at 19:30. So much for pre-warning them that I might be late.

No help for that. All I could do was trundle onward. And upward. The road had some stiff gradients to contend with. At least, in the dark and with tired legs they felt like stiff gradients.

At one point I passed a sign showing Tomatin 5 Inverness 25. That was a welcome relief; Tomatin was the town I was heading for and Inverness the first major town for tomorrow. I was nearly there.

Half a mile later there was another sign: Tomatin 6 Inverness 23! So somehow, despite being in the same direction and on the same route, I had managed

**184**

to cycle one mile further away from Tomatin but two miles closer to Inverness?

Nevertheless, I eventually crested the Slog It Summit and the last 5 miles were downhill, other than a little off route upward kick at the end to reach the B&B.

I parked my bike around the side of the B&B and hauled my bags and bits to the door. I tried to look lost and pathetic when I rang the bell. I didn't need to try and look tired.

The landlady was made of stern stuff though and was unimpressed. I resorted to dialogue and expressed my apologies for being late, explaining that my route had proved to be 15 miles further than expected and that I had lost some time fixing a puncture. Otherwise I would have been 2 hours earlier.

She thawed slightly so I pressed the attack saying that, if it would be easier, I could just dump my bags in my room and come straight to dinner in my cycling kit.

Yes, that would be fine.

Ironically I had sent a change of clothes in my parcel for this B&B, knowing that I would be eating here and not wanting to sit in a sweaty cycling kit. All that forethought managed to do was load me with an extra kilo of baggage for the last and longest push to the finish the next day.

By the end of the meal the landlady had thawed out completely and was willing to leave out breakfast for an early start in the morning. My average speed, including all stops, was still about 10 mph so I would need 14 hours for the last day. I was hoping to leave by 07:00 which would mean a finish around 21:00.

I was amazed to note that my total ascent had

been under 1,500m. If I had been riding in Devon I could have expected to have climbed at least 2,500m over 124 miles. I was again impressed with how well the Scottish road builders dealt with their hills.

| Distance: | 124 miles | Av speed: | 13.9 mph |
|---|---|---|---|
| Time cycling: | 8:52 | Time overall: | 12:05 |
| Av heart rate: | 132 bpm | Calories burnt: | 4,237 |
| Total ascent: | 1,489 m | Max speed: | 45.0 mph |

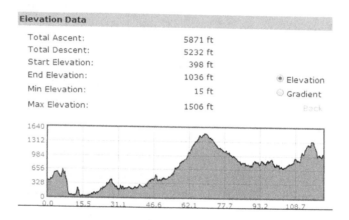

# Chapter Thirteen

## Day 8 – TA DA!!!

The last push. The final countdown. The final hoorah! Once more unto the breach, dear friends, once more; or close the wall up with our English dead. In peace there's nothing so becomes a man as modest stillness and humility: but when the blast of war blows in our ears, then imitate the action of the tiger; stiffen the sinews, summon up the blood...

Sorry, I seemed to have woken up as Henry V.

But I was feeling like a greyhound in the slips, straining upon the start. For the game was afoot. One more effort.

Yes!! I managed to turn the beeping alarm off.

Though groggy and stiff I managed to stumble about fairly rapidly, the adrenaline already starting to permeate the fog in my head. In record time I gathered all my bits and pieces together and tip toed down the stairs and into the dining room.

After champing stolidly through a large bowl of muesli and washing it down with a pint of orange juice I sneaked out the front door and crept around the side of the house to grab my bike.

It was still dark so I lit up front and rear and gently slipped away, initially retracing my route of the night before, this time thankfully downhill back to the main road. I had managed to get away in record time and was on the main route a few minutes after half past six.

There were a few ups and down but overall the first

15 miles was notably downhill. I had started at over 300m and the Kessock Bridge (just north of Inverness) was at sea level. I used up all my stored climbing energy but managed to average about 15mph, even with a couple of stops. If I had kept that up I would have been in John O'Groats by 4pm! However, if I had continued to descend an aggregate 300m every 15 miles I would also have been 2,500m below sea level at the end and I was sure John O'Groats was by the sea, not at the bottom of a mine.

The Beauly Firth provided a magnificent backdrop to the bridge crossing, everything steely grey in the dawn light, the clouds reflected in the flat calm water. They were pretty solid clouds but at least they weren't showing any signs of precipitating on me just yet.

Beyond the bridge I followed National Cycle Route 1. I would follow it as far as the Dornoch Firth. However, about 4 miles after the bridge NCR 1 splits. The part I didn't follow heads to Cromarty where a ferry awaits to transport cars, cycles and passenger across the mouth of the Cromarty Firth to Nigg on the opposite shore and thence to join back with the part I followed in Tarn. I was sticking to the land route because I didn't want to lose time by just missing a crossing when I had 140 miles to cover.

At one point the route came close to the A9 and I discovered a car by the side of the road on its roof. It had clearly rolled for a bit before coming to rest and was now bedecked with police tape. It is a dangerous place being on the A9. I took some photos but they seemed to have disappeared from my folder. Mysterious. Perhaps the police have hacked in and deleted photos I was not meant to take. Spooky. They didn't get the one of the police car on day 3 though. Ha!

By 8:00 the clouds had come down to sit on my head. With little to see my attention was drawn back to signs by the road. There was an interesting one for 'Surgery Free Church'. That had me confused. Perhaps it was a religion you could convert to without a lobotomy? It took me a while to realise that Surgery and Free Church had been on two separate lines and were perhaps two separate things. In my defence, I was majorly fatigued by that stage.

Another intriguing sign was one at Tore Burial Ground (no mere cemetery for Tore) stating 'no dogs allowed'. Maybe they had their own burial ground somewhere else.

28 miles in, I stopped at Dingwall and topped up on drinks. Whilst it was still early in the day I treated myself to a caffeine drink and a bar of chocolate to help focus my wandering mind.

I used up the sugar almost immediately battling the stiff climb out of town. Despite my best efforts to not exert myself I built up a quite a sweat. It should be pointed out that after eight days in the saddle my hairy growth was starting to get itchy so when I got to the top and could release a hand from the handlebars I indulged in a quick scratch. Well, you know how it is when you start scratching – pretty soon my stubby beard was itching too. Very irritating but easier to scratch.

At 9:20 I phoned home, needing to hear a friendly

voice: I was getting very lonely by now. My average speed had dropped but was still over 12mph, having covered 34 miles in roughly 2 hours 45 minutes. That still left over a hundred miles to go though.

Fortunately the fog had lifted and I was able to enjoy the scenery once more. I was mainly rolling through arable farmland and was pleased to see that the Scottish farmers of the far north had spurned the need to clad their hay bales in black plastic. The cotton reels were left naked and unfettered, free to gambol in the fields, as they should be.

The road was very quiet. I was on a minor road ghosting roughly along the path of the A9. I had seen maybe a couple of cars an hour, no more. Ironically though, just as I pulled over to relieve the boredom and the pressure from my bladder a succession of cars decided to make an appearance, obviously having

hidden around the corner all day awaiting their opportunity.

As I waited for them to pass I was disappointed to spot what was possibly the world's longest hay bale, all encased in black plastic. I'm not sure that the farmer had set up his baling machine correctly because it looked more like a swiss roll. A not very appetising liquorice covered swiss roll. Perhaps the idea was to slice a chunk off every time he needed some more?

With the coast clear I did what I needed to do and pushed off once more. Half way down a glorious descent I joined the A9 and continued downhill as it skirted around Tain towards the Dornoch Firth. I was now going to be on the A9 for the next 57 miles until I turned off onto minor roads, 30 miles short of the finish. Fortunately the A9 was quiet and there was a decent amount of tarmac beyond the rumble strip to ride on.

My spirits were lifted first by the sign for Glenmorangie (perfected by the sixteen men of Tain: that's men for you – takes sixteen of them to get

anything right!), where I was tempted to pop in for a tasting and then, just before the Dornoch Firth Bridge, by my first sighting of a John O'Groats sign: 85 miles to go!

The Dornoch Firth marked a milestone: 1400km cycled since I had started (perhaps that should be a kilometrestone but it doesn't have the same ring to it though). That was the distance of LEL. So I had covered the same distance. Woo hoo! It had taken 2 ½ days more than the 5 days allowed though. Boo hoo!

Ach! I was long past the need to fulfil the hole left by the disappointment of DNF on LEL. I was having the most wonderful time, riding at a sensible pace across the country, taking the time to enjoy the areas I was passing through. The sun was shining on my head (metaphorically at least) and I was at peace with the world. Who could not be with glorious view of the Dornoch Firth, resplendent in autumn colour, stretching out before them?

I was still managing to average about 12mph, being 60 miles and 5 hours into the day. Having averaged about 10 mph across the rest of the country it was puzzling to be 20% faster today. I had climbed 660m so it wasn't because it was flat, although I had used that 300m of stored climbing

energy. It was most likely that I was subconsciously giving it a bit more today, knowing that I didn't have to get back on the bike tomorrow. I warned myself not to overdo it in case I burned out before the end. I still had 80+ miles to go.

On the other side of the Dornoch Firth was Sutherland. It was twinned with Zetel. I had forgotten about my, 'Who Can Spot The Scottish Place Name With The Highest Scrabble Score' game. Although Zetel did not score highly (14) it had caught my eye because of the Z. Of course technically it wasn't a Scottish place name: Zetel is a municipality in the district of Friesland, Lower Saxony, Germany (full address 65!).

Almost immediately I also used up an X: River Evelix (24).

There were no houses after the sign for Sutherland. I cycled on and on

and found none. Where were all the people in this town? I wondered if nobody lived in Zetel either. Or perhaps everyone had moved to Zetel? Or more sensibly: maybe the road had bypassed the town?

It was only later that I realised Sutherland was a county not a town. Durh! But then I'd never heard of counties being twinned. Although perhaps I should have because it appears my home county of Devon is the only English county to be twinned with a county in France: Calvados, famous for its apple brandy. I wonder why those Devon dignitaries chose that region?

I also learnt that Sutherland derives from Old Norse for Southern Land, which initially puzzled me, it being at the most northern part of mainland Scotland. However the Norse settlements were centred in Orkney so the term was relative.

As I pedalled further north the A9 became quieter and quieter. There were few cars and fewer lorries. It was like following a river to its source: each time I passed a tributary road the traffic flow became less.

The other thing than reduced as I headed north was the height of the buildings. The further I went the more predominant bungalows became. There are probably very practical reasons for this. The cost of land is probably not excessive enough to necessitate the need for building upward instead of outward. Also I'm sure lower buildings provide better shelter against severe weather conditions. But being perverse by nature I wondered whether there was some hobbit blood in the denizens of the far north. No going upstairs for the wild northern Scot: bedrooms, bathrooms, cellars, pantries (lots of these), wardrobes, kitchens, dining-rooms, all were on the same floor – to misquote Tolkien.

My mind was wandering but just before noon I was put on my toes. Otter Warning! Dang! I thought I'd left the wee beasties with the nasty pointy teeth back in the Cairngorms. Now it seemed Sutherland had its own version. I would have to be vigilant.

Approaching Loch Fleet I had my eyes peeled. Loch = water. Water = otters. They weren't going to sneak up on this soldier!

I risked stopping to take a

picture of the loch then climbed up and over the hill to Golspie, well out of otter range. To celebrate my successful evasion and the fact that I was very nearly halfway I bought a caffeine drink and filled one of my bottles with it.

From miles before Golspie a monument had been visible on the hill above the town. In fact I first spotted it descending to Tain about 18 miles back. Now, having left the town, I realised that I had lost my opportunity of asking a local about it. Googling it when I got home I discovered it was a 100 foot tall statue of George Granville Leveson-Gower, Marquess of Stafford and first Duke of Sutherland.

He became notorious because of the part he played in the Highland clearances, although his reputation depends upon whom you talk to. Supporters state that when he arrived in the Highlands, after his marriage to the daughter of the Earl of Sutherland, he was appalled at the conditions his tenants were living in. He became convinced that the interior of Sutherland could not support these subsistence farmers long term. He decided to resettle the population in new villages along the coast where they had a greater opportunity of eking a living. The more common view is that he decided it would be more profitable for the estate to turn the land over to large scale sheep farming, so the tenants would have to go, whether they wanted to or not.

Either way, these reforms led to thousands of people being evicted from their homes and farms, many of them forcefully. It was not unknown for overzealous enforcers to burn villages to the ground.

Even today feelings still run high and the statue has suffered from graffiti and several blocks have been removed from the plinth in an attempt to topple it. There have been calls for it to be removed and a monument in memory of the evicted tenants to be erected in its place.

It was a shame I didn't have this to occupy my mind as I cranked my way up the climb out of Golspie. For instance, I would have known that Dunrobin Castle, which I passed near the top of the climb, was the ancestral home of the Earls of Sutherland. Instead I was left to wonder at the audacity of the name. There are plenty of homes called Dunroamin but it seemed to be flaunting it a bit to call your house Dunrobin, after you've pillaged the neighbourhood and set yourself up as Earl.

Opposite the entrance to the castle is the entrance to Dunrobin Railway Station. Having watched Michael Portilio

Dunrobin Castle

visit the station on his Great Railway Journeys program I decided to stop and have a look. I needed a wee anyway. Unfortunately it was all closed up: obviously I was not as important as Mr Portilio. But it was very picturesque.

Remounting the bike I took a long slug of drink before setting off again and had my own Highland clearance experience. The gas from the caffeine drink had built to enormous pressure in my bottle and the moment I pulled the valve open with my teeth it exploded into my mouth and forcefully evicted everything that was clinging to the inside of my nostrils.

A little further down the road I pulled onto an overgrown lane for a much needed wee. There I found further evidence of Hobbit genes in the Highlanders DNA: a half buried bungalow; a semi burrow. The further north I travelled the stronger the evidence was becoming. Perhaps, if I could catch a Highlander with their shoes off, I could check for thick curly hair on their feet.

The A9 bounced up and down a bit and I wondered why I had thought it so flat when I had ridden the other way. I reasoned it was because 1) I was fitter then; 2) I had fresh legs and 3) my expectation was for much worse. Now my legs were

fatigued and my expectation was for flat.

Just before reaching Helmsdale my bike started making an annoying noise. It wasn't really a creak; it was deeper than that. It wasn't regular either. I tried not pedalling but the noise continued, so deduced it had nothing to do with the vital drive unit. I bounced on the saddle (as much as by butt would allow) but this did not cause the noise, so it wasn't the seat post or the saddle coming loose. I pulled on the handlebars but this got no reaction. Puzzled I stopped to see if anything was rubbing anywhere. The last thing I needed was a major mechanical within spitting distance of the finish. Without the background noises of cycling it was obvious the noise was not coming from the bike. It was the sound of waves rolling up the beach not far to my right.

I texted home with a lame joke, probably made by anybody who has been to Helmsdale and read Lord of the Rings.

*14:03 In Helms Deep. A sea of orcs crashing against the walls. Oh no. Hang on, Helmsdale! And just the sea crashing against the wall. Major climb after this.*

My wife wasn't impressed. She responded that I had made the same joke last time and it wasn't funny then either. Actually I think last time I had said I was searching for Legolas and Gimli to tell them my orc kill count was 44!

As you roll into Helmsdale you get no indication of the climb to come but after crossing the Helmsdale River you almost immediately start to climb steeply whilst still in the town. It was only foreknowledge that allowed me to re-adjust my expectations for a gruelling climb. Foreknowledge also had me turning off into town to stock up on drinks because I couldn't remember any shops between here and Wick from my last trip. I wasn't going through Wick this time so expected it this might have been my last chance to top up.

In the shop I was faced with a choice of buying a 2 litre bottle of drink on offer for £1 or a 500ml bottle of the same drink for £1.49. I only needed 500ml. My dilemma was did I waste 49p or 1½ litres of drink? Tight as a tourniquet (thanks Pink Floyd) I was soon pouring drink down the drain.

As I was doing so a couple of young and trendy kids were walking down the street. One turned to go into the shop and by way of farewell said to the other, "Laters." The bizarre response was, "See you soon alligator." This was either some new cult farewell, deliberately designed to irritate the old, or the traditional phrase had not travelled well on the way north.

I now had two full bottles on the bike and had drunk as much of the spare 1½ litres as I could. It was a weight off my mind to be fully stocked but was also a considerable extra weight on my bike. Heavily laden I set off up the infamous hill.

Having adjusted my expectation for the hill it didn't prove to be too bad. The worst part was the first ramp, getting out of town, which was fairly steady at 8/9%. The road then rolled up and down a little before a second ramp of 7/8%, a short respite and then a 3rd ramp starting at 6% and ending at 9%. After that is a short section of false flat around a hairpin bend and them a final ramp of 2/3%.

The hill did grind on for a long time though. From the bridge at the bottom it was about 3½ miles to the top but on the final ramp I was rewarded by passing into Caithness, the final county on my cycle across the country.

At the top I was feeling quite sick. First of all I put it down to the climb but after descending the other side (much shorter) and rolling along a little I still felt bad.

Stopping I realised my body was feeling shaky. I wasn't physically shaking but my limbs felt decidedly buzzy. I had overdosed on caffeine through the day and was now starting to suffer from the consequences. The problem I faced was that one of my bottles was full of caffeine drink. I didn't want to have any more so that left me with one bottle with 50 miles to go.

By chance I had stopped at a sign for Badhea Clearance Village. Even in my shaky state I had enough logical reasoning left to surmise that this must have had something to do with the Highland Clearances and was not a discount retail outlet, like Clarks Village in Somerset.

In an effort to stop the shaking I took a break from cycling and explored instead. A short walk down the path brought me to the ruins of a village. It had been established after the local crofters had been cleared from the surrounding area to make room for large scale sheep farms. The evicted tenants were given a plot of land but had to clear it

themselves and build their own homes from the stones they found. The land itself was very poor, sloping down to a cliff edge. Not an area in which anyone would choose to live if they had to make their living from the land. Ultimately that is what happened: the last tenant moved away in 1911 but most had left long before. Standing resolutely against the elements was a stone monument erected to commemorate the people of Badhea. It was raised by the son of one for the former tenants who had emigrated to New Zeal-and in 1839 on the site of his grandfather's house.

My walk about hadn't helped and I was still feeling queasy so I got on my bike and tried to cycle through it instead.

Before I knew it I was plunging down the Berriedale Braes descent. This is proper steep. As is the ascent which starts immediately after crossing the bridge that spans both the Berriedale Water and Langwell Water rivers, just before they converge.

The sign at the bottom warns of a 13% gradient. Fortunately it was not quite that bad. My sat nav registered 11% on the hairpin bend near the bottom but after that it was a fairly steady 10%. With tired legs and a loaded bike 10% is a considerable challenge though, especially with Helmsdale climb still fresh in the legs. Just as I was beginning to feel like dying, a handy cemetery appeared on the left. It was the beginning of the end. Shortly after the gradient eased off to 7/8%, which it maintained to the top, about a mile from the bridge.

I texted home from the top to say that the big hills were done and I had completed 96 miles in just under 9 hrs. So I was still over my customary 10 mph but the hills had eaten away at  the average speed I had been achieving earlier in the day.

Still feeling sick I reasoned that maybe eating something would help. Pulling up alongside some Aberdeen Anguses (the only ones I had seen on this trip) I dug some sausage rolls and crisps out of my bag. It took a fair amount of willpower to get them down. It felt like kill or cure. I also drained the last of my non caffeine bottle and prayed that I'd find a shop.

The road was easier going now with shallower undulations allowing me to chug along without having to put big efforts in on the hills. Ahead of me I could see headland after headland stretching away into the distance, merging with the horizon. It was daunting to think that my destination was, at the very least, the furthest point I could see. My sat nav was telling me I had 30 miles to go, which meant I had covered 110 miles so far that day. Seeing what might have been only about 20 miles disappearing beyond the horizon gave me some appreciation of just how far I had travelled. Over the last eight days I had cycled to that horizon the best part of fifty times. Just one more to go. Once more unto the breach, dear friends, once more; or close the wall...don't start that again!

My prayer requesting a shop was answered, albeit 45 minutes later when I was getting thirsty enough to start thinking about trying the caffeine drink. I found a shop in Lybster, a tiny town that was once a big herring fishing port and now has possibly the widest high street in the country! I have no idea what that was about. But the shop was heaven sent. I bought water. Lots of water. I drank as much as I could to try and flush out my system and then emptied my bottles of poison, rinsed them and filled them with pure clean water.

Already feeling much better I set off on the last 32 miles.

A mile down the main road, which had become the A99 a few miles back in Latheron, I turned onto a minor road. This far north the main road was fairly minor itself but this new road was single track with no room for passing. But that didn't matter, there was only me on it.

The road was arrow straight and very gently rolling, just about 1-2%. With a tailwind to assist me I cruised down the downs and then used my momentum to carry me up the ups. I could see the road stretching out before me but I was eating it up.

In fact I was cruising along so well I almost missed the final evidence I needed to prove my Hobbit DNA theory. A hundred metres off the road was what looked very much like a Hobbit house, or at least the type of house a Hobbit would build if there was no convenient hillside to dig into. True, there were signs stating that it was a cairn used for burials and rituals about 5,000 years ago but you only had to look at the height of the door to know it was built by a Hobbit. Archaeologists just guess most of the time.

The excitement was coming thick and fast in the last few miles. Literally around the corner I entered a forest, not of trees but windmills. The sound they made was awesome. Or to use a word from Tyger Pants, a character in one of the children's books I write – awefull (if something that leaves you in *some* awe is awe*some* then something that leaves you *full* of awe must be awe*full*, right?). And up close they are just magnificent. Massive.

Despite stopping several times to take pictures of the windmills the miles were zipping away. The sun even came out for a final farewell and I snapped a picture of my shadow, who I hadn't seen all day.

Feeling devilish with 15 miles to go I stopped to text home: *17:50 At a standstill.* I followed it up with: *Oh no, sorry! In Stanstill. 15 to go but just hit off road section!*

My last off road section was a farm track. It was pretty bumpy and not exactly what certain parts of my anatomy would have ordered up, given the choice. In fact, despite the poor reputation of its cuisine, other than the fish supper in Lockerbie, the only battered thing I had had whilst in Scotland was battered butt.

Battered Butt was the least of my worries though. Stretched across my path were some pipes. These were not small pipes. Oh no. These pipes were about five feet in diameter and held about a foot above the ground on some kind of rail system. There was no chance of skirting around them, they stretched as far as I could see in both directions. Can't go under it, can't go around it, can't go through it – have to go over it.

It was a stretch to lift he bike over and lower it as gently as possible to the ground the other side. It was even more of a stretch, and a major threat to cramp in tired limbs, to scramble over the slippery plastic pipe. All to be repeated 10 metres further on where another pipe awaited.

My athletic performance was watched from afar by two local men flying a kite in a field. There were no children in evidence so I had to assume that the entertainment possibilities that far north were limited. They took great delight in pointing out that if I had stayed on the road I could have avoided having to cross

the pipes. And it would have been shorter. I mumbled something incoherent and pointed at my sat nav. Didn't they understand my mission was to follow the route, no matter what (unless it went through a house or river)?

I later looked the area up on Google Map and have to report that the locals were correct. There is no logical explanation why Google routed me the way it did, unless there's a computer somewhere with a 'bloody minded sense of humour' chip...a chip on its shoulder for bike routes?

To save face I gathered the last of my dignity around me like a cloak and cycled off at speed. Unfortunately I went the wrong way so I had to scuttle back a couple of minutes later.

The last few miles were: long straight road, little wiggle, long straight road, little wiggle, long straight road, few wiggles – Ta Dah!

But it took a long time to get to Ta Dah! The light was fading fast and so was the energy in my legs. The long straight roads stretched on and on. At one point, on a slight rise, I could see a measured 2 miles of road behind me. Turning 180 degrees, in a dead straight line before me was an even longer stretch of road, disappearing over the next slight rise in the distance. There was a whole lot of nothing much to see apart from the telegraph poles with their swagged wires keeping the road company on its journey north.

By the time I had reached the last couple of miles I just wanted it to end. There was no bubbling up of euphoria at the prospect of reaching my goal. I had turned into the wind and was limping to the finish line rather than sprinting. My eyes dropped to my sat nav which was already reading 140+ miles. I should have already been there. Keeping my head down, out of the wind, I watched the distance tick very slowly up. Never a good thing mentally.

Finally I reached a T junction and turned towards the finish. Suddenly the wind was behind me again and it was all downhill from here. Spirits soaring I plunged down the hill, swooped around the final bend in the road and raised my hands in triumph to salute the screaming crowd pressed 5 deep up against the barriers, waving their huge foam hands and thumping the sponsors advertising boards.

Ok, that's not strictly true: I don't like taking both hands off the handlebars and there was no bugger around. Not even a seagull. But then it was getting dark and who gives a toss about another cyclist reaching John O'Groats, apart from the rider themselves and maybe their family and friends?

The finish was a bit of an anti-climax. The main problem with riding solo is that you have no one to share the experience with, at least not directly, in the moment. I did manage an effusive email though that let all the emotion out in a torrent of words: *TA DA!!!* Three exclamation marks is a clear sign of emotional excitement (four for emotional instability and five for barking).

It was 18:53, which meant I had covered the last 15 miles in just over an hour. That tailwind had help me considerably because it had felt like I was crawling. And that is all I wanted to do at that point, crawl to my B&B, shower and then call home.

It was a good plan only thwarted by the lack of signal at the B&B. I managed to get a text out but the signal was not consistent enough for a call. Very frustrating. In fact it was only the next day I managed to make contact when I cycled back to the signpost to take photos.

The frustration comes across in my texts and the blog post from my wife:

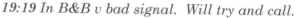

*19:19 In B&B v bad signal. Will try and call.*

*Sunday, 07:34  Have tried calling several times but it just keeps cutting me off. Bugger! Got to finish just before 7. As good as dark. Tummy not good. Too much caffeine. Last 30 miles fantastic. Very straight single track, tarmacked roads which wavered up and down 1 - 2 %. Very fast although legs were tired.*

*07:40 I've only just managed to send a text from last night. No signal as I type this but will send once I get one. Tummy still fairly liquid. Glad I'm not riding today! Knee quite painful but can walk on it ok. Breakfast at 8 then try and pack everything into bag. Might need some careful thinking! I'll then head back to the signpost to see if I can get a better picture.*

*It was a very bad signal - I didn't get to talk to Roy for a celebratory "Hooray"! Very frustrating! But he's done it. And made good time today, despite the miles in his legs. Arrived well before 20:00. How's that for a flourishing finish? Hoorah!!! Hoorah!!!! Hoorah!!!!!* [What did I say about exclamation marks?]

It also served to remind me that my stomach was suffering horribly from my caffeine overdose. With the passage of time I had forgotten about that. The human brain is very good at that sort of thing. It's why we are able to do crazy stuff more than once. After a thoroughly miserable time slogging through cold and rain, up nasty steep gradients and down narrow twisting descents with gravel and crap strewn across them, we only remember the thrill of getting up those hills and finishing the ride. Expunged from the memory banks (or at least locked away) are the curses and swearing and the vows never to try doing this stupid bloody ride again. It's also the reason families have more than one child.

Whilst I was at the signpost the next morning, killing time waiting for my pre-arranged lift to Inverness and taking photos in case the ones from the previous evening's gloaming did not come out, a man with a pushchair arrived.

He spent some time loading the pushchair with bags and cameras and even a full sized tripod, then approached the signpost where his lift buddy took a few photos. Intrigued I wandered over and asked what his mission was. His name was Chris and he was running to Land's End, pushing his luggage, attempting to complete 35 marathons over 40 days. The trip was a warm up test before his planned attempt to run around the world. And I subtitled my trip 'Roy's Mad Adventure'? It's all relative.

| | | | |
|---|---|---|---|
| Distance: | 142 miles | Av speed: | 14.5 mph |
| Time cycling: | 9:47 | Time overall: | 12:27 |
| Av heart rate: | 128 bpm | Calories burnt: | 4,363 |
| Total ascent: | 1,836 m | Max speed: | 44.3 mph |

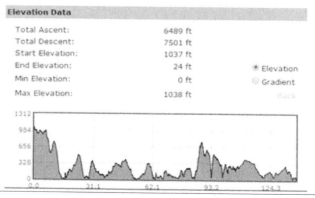

# Chapter Fourteen

## Epilogue

The time immediately after the ride is probably best summed up by the blog post I made a few days later.

### So That's That

It's now a few days since the end. That sounds ominous - perhaps 'since the finish' would be better. I'm feeling a bit more tired every day but other than that really good. Apart from the dodgy knee. And I'm sure that will also be fine in a couple of days.

Huge thanks to my lovely wife, Jocelyn, who has kept the house together, the family alive and (more importantly) the blog running so excellently well. And much thanks to my mother who came down to stay and help out whilst I was on the road (well quite a bit of off road actually but you know what I mean).

One of the things that struck me on this route was the stark contrast between cycling peacefully along a canal path with nothing but ducks for company and then being instantly dumped on a frenetic A road, with cars and lorries rumbling past, rattling your teeth. It's a good analogy for coming back home. You go from not having to think about anything other than pedalling, eating, drinking and sleeping to being bombarded with questions, demands, information and tasks. They are normally there all the time but you grow so used to them you don't necessarily notice. When you've been out of real life for a while it hits you like a train.

My trip back to home (Ivybridge nr Plymouth) was long but nowhere near as long as the one up. The John O'Groats Bike Transport Company picked me (and my bike) up from JOG at 10:00am on Sunday and whizzed me down to Inverness. They dropped me at the airport and took my bike away to be boxed up and couriered to my house. The bike was dispatched the next day and arrived the day after that, just in time to be cleaned, oiled and greased ready for commuting to work today.

I have to say I think it is the best solution to getting back from JOG if you haven't got a support vehicle following you. The John O'Groats Bike Transport Company do a fantastic job at getting you to Inverness and then you can select plane (my recommended option), train or one way hire car from there.

I had to spend a few hours in the airport but after 8 days of cycling, sitting around is no bad thing. Whilst the view of my feet wasn't inspiring I did get to use my mp3 player for the first time, justifying carrying it right across the country. That in itself is a good indication of how the trip went because I had brought it with me to lift my mood if things got too tough.

After the hours of waiting it was just a 50 minute hop to Manchester and a similar one on to Exeter where I was reunited with my lovely wife. Not being a frequent air traveller I still get excited

about being on a plane. It is a rare opportunity to look at the world from another perspective and a reminder that above the clouds the sun is always shining [at least in the day] waiting to break through. A good metaphor for life.

This was a terrific trip which I thoroughly enjoyed. I think the Google map route was excellent. It could be improved by re-routing a couple of sections, which I will endeavour to do. Of course, I was on a racing geometry road bike - the only concession I made to the route was to use 25 mm Schwalbe Marathon tyres. If you rode an off road bike, a hybrid or a tour bike it would be even more doable. However, there are several places where you have to lift the bike up to shoulder level so you would need to consider that.

All in all though - well done Google Maps on your bicycle routing!

# Final Thoughts

On the first day I had told myself to relax and enjoy the ride. It worked: I *really* enjoyed the ride. So much so that I want to share it as a guide. I will have to re-route the dodgy bits and then re-ride it to make sure it works of course (any excuse).

I had thought that my strong mental attitude had helped me to stop worrying about the time and to just twiddle and enjoy the ride but it was more likely the route.

On my first end to end I had been time driven, needing to devour the miles each day. But with nothing of interest to see on the main roads there wasn't anything to distract me from that mission. In evidence of that is the fact that I wasn't inspired to stop and take a single photo between the Scotland sign on the border and the Clifton Suspension Bridge in Bristol. That's most of England.

In contrast, this route provided an ever changing and beautiful scene that I didn't want to race through. I wanted to take the time to enjoy the sights I was seeing, living in the moment and not worrying about where I should be in an hour, two hours down the road. On the whole I remember smiling a lot, at least inwardly.

But did I achieve my goal? Did I banish the LEL demons and prove I was fit enough to have completed the ride?

Ultimately we are all only accountable to one person. Many people around the world will say that person is God, in whatever form she may take. For me, the person you are accountable to is yourself. The only person putting you through an emotional roller coaster is you. The person who generates those feelings of love, hate, joy, guilt, depression, panic, euphoria...is you. Sure, they are triggered by some external thing but the emotions are all self-contained.

The emotions I felt after failing to complete LEL were mine to deal with. I had felt inclined to blame it all on the lorry driver. It was his fault I was feeling like that. Actually no. It was his fault I had been injured but it was my fault I was feeling how I was. I could have looked at it pragmatically and concluded that 'it is what it is' and moved on.

To deal with the emotion I, quite logically, devised a different challenge to satisfy the demons and prove that all was well. In the event, the challenge was different to LEL. True the distance was the same but the time pressure was not. LEJOG was easier but at the end the demons were gone. In reality the demons had mostly fled by the time I pedalled away from Land's End, washed away in a flood of activity to organise the ride. And they were completely banished on day six when the hills to Edinburgh never materialised.

That was a strange feeling. On one side of the scale I was annoyed because it meant the LEL course was not as bad as I had thought, which meant my decision to turn back was wrong. Out weighing that on the other side was a feeling that I definitely could have finished the ride if my knee hadn't been a factor. Of course, I will never know the true answer.

Somewhere deep in my system I can still feel a demon seed lurking though. The next LEL is 2017. I'll be fifty in 2017. That deserves a celebratory challenge doesn't it? Something to disavow the onslaught of age. I wonder...

# Other Books

## Self Help Guide

If this book has inspired you to take up the challenge of riding from Land's End to John O'Groats yourself then you may be interested in Royston's: Land's End to John O'Groats Self Help Cycle Guide.

The guide has helped thousands of readers with tips and advice about:

- How to get to the start/from the finish
- Where you are going to sleep
- Equipment - what you need to take with you
- Nutrition - what you should eat and drink
- How much training you need to do
- Route creation including how to create your own personalised route with gpx file using Google Maps

The book is available as:

Paperback at Amazon
Kindle at Amazon
E book at iBooks
E book at Smashwords
PDF at www.landsend-to-johnogroats.co.uk

Also available worldwide from various online retailers.

Land's End
to
John O'Groats
Self Help Cycle Guide

# End to End Cycle Route

Also available is Royston's 'Safe' Cycle Route. It is based on the route cycled in this book but with all the bits he moaned about re-routed (and then re-ridden to test it).

It is a set of 18 gpx route files that use quiet roads and lanes, cycle paths, old railway lines and tow paths to guide you from one end of the country to the other. The gpx files are accompanied by a book to tell you how to use and amend them together with lists of accommodation and cycle shops and maps.

The book is available as:

> Paperback at Amazon
> Kindle at Amazon
> PDF at www.landsend-to-johnogroats.co.uk

CPSIA information can be obtained
at www.ICGtesting.com
Printed in the USA
LVOW04s1454121216

516919LV0004TB/3/109/P

9 781500 370893